Forged In Fire

The Industrial Legacy of Appalachia's Highlands

By Daine Mackey

447 Broadway
2nd Floor
New York, NY 10013

Staten House Publishing

Forged In Fire: The Industrial Legacy of Appalachia's Highlands

Copyright © 2024 by Daine Mackey

All rights reserved. Thank you for your purchase of this book, I ask that you please adhere to my legal request that no part of this publication may be reproduced in any form, or by any means, electronic or mechanical, including photocopying, recording, or any information browsing, storage, or retrieval system without express written permission by the author, except in the case of brief brief quotations embodied within reviews and certain non-commercial uses permitted by law. Educational use and use with, for, or within public displays for the purpose of educating the public in or outside of a public or private museum setting must be properly and fully cited.

ISBN 979-8-89496-859-9

Library of Congress Control Number: 2024917958

First Edition 2024

For my fantastic son who brings life to my life who inspire me every day with his boundless intelligence and curiosities. This book is also dedicated to all those both within the region and abroad who are connected to these historical places and keep their existence alive both physically and in memory.

Special thanks to Brandon Gerding for his photographical prowess.

*Thanks as well to these characters and **all others** in my life and in these areas:*

Jesus, Chris Greene, Mr. Crawford, Jeffrey Wilson, Karl Sanchez, & of course the Jesse Stuart Foundation who provides continual support of arts & literature in the region.

Table of contents

Chapter 1: Bedrock and Bounty: The Geological Foundations of the Hanging Rock Iron Region   4

Chapter 2: River of Progress: The Ohio's Role in Shaping the Iron Industry   14

Chapter 3: From Earth to Furnace: The Journey of Iron Ore in Hanging Rock   22

Chapter 4: Amanda's Flame: The Rise and Fall of Amanda Furnace   26

Chapter 5: Buckeye's Legacy: The Story of Buckeye Furnace and Its Community   35

Chapter 6: Cambria's Crucible: Shaping Lives in the Shadow of the Furnace   43

Chapter 7: Gallia's Glow: The History of Gallia Furnace   50

Chapter 8: Huron's Heritage: The Chronicle of Huron Furnace   59

Chapter 9: Jefferson's Journey: The Saga of Jefferson Furnace   69

Chapter 10: Lawrence's Labor: The Chronicle of Lawrence Furnace   78

Chapter 11: Iron Siblings: Madison and Monroe Furnaces' Shared Heritage   87

Chapter 12: Olive's Offering: The Narrative of Olive Furnace   97

Chapter 13: Union's Unity: The History of Union Furnace   107

Chapter 14: Vesuvius Rises: The Story of Vesuvius Furnace   117

Chapter 15: Washington's Will: The Tale of Washington Furnace   127

Chapter 16: Center Stage: The History of Center Furnace   136

Chapter 17: Etna's Epoch: The Legacy of Etna Furnace   139

Chapter 18: Hearths and Homes: Life in the Iron Furnace Company Towns   148

Chapter 19: Iron's Eternal Echo: The Lasting Legacy of The Hanging Rock Iron Region   168

Introduction

Forged in Fire: An Overview of Appalachia's Industrial Legacy

In the heart of Appalachia, where the rolling hills and verdant forests of Ohio, Kentucky, and West Virginia converge, lies a region that has been forged by the relentless pursuit of progress and the unyielding spirit of its people. The Hanging Rock Iron Region, a name that echoes through the annals of American industrial history, is a testament to the ingenuity, determination, and resilience of those who have shaped this land for generations.

"Forged in Fire: The Industrial Legacy of Appalachia's Highlands" is a minimalist collection of remaining information still available, and thorough journey through the rich and complex history of the Hanging Rock Iron Region, a land where the echoes of ancient civilizations and the thunder of 19th-century industry intertwine in a tapestry of human achievement. From the area of the enigmatic mounds and earthworks of the ancient cultures to the towering blast furnaces that once lit the night sky, this book explores the diverse and interconnected stories that have shaped this remarkable region.

As we embark on this exploration, we begin by delving into the deep geological history of the Appalachian Mountains, the very foundation upon which the Hanging Rock Iron Region was built. Chapter 1 takes us on a journey through the eons, from the formation of ancient oceans and the collision of continents to the creation of the vast mineral deposits that would one day fuel the region's industrial might. We discover the rich coal seams and iron ore deposits that have been both a blessing and a curse, shaping the lives and livelihoods of countless generations.

In Chapter 2, we turn our attention to the lifeblood of the region—the mighty Ohio River and its tributaries. These waterways have been the arteries of commerce and transportation, connecting the Hanging Rock Iron Region to the wider world and facilitating the growth of industry and trade. From the early days of Native American canoe travel to the golden age of steamboats and barges, the rivers have played a central role in the region's development and prosperity.

As we continue our journey, Chapter 3 delves into the intricacies of iron ore mining and transportation, the very foundation of the Hanging Rock Iron Region's industrial success. We explore the backbreaking labor of the miners, the ingenious methods of extraction, and the complex networks of railroads and canals that carried the precious ore to the waiting furnaces. Through the stories of the men and women who toiled in the mines and on the transportation routes, we gain a deeper appreciation for the sacrifices and determination that built this region.

Chapters 4 through 16 take us on a fascinating tour of the individual furnaces that once dotted the landscape of the Hanging Rock Iron Region. From the pioneering Amanda Furnace to the towering Vesuvius Furnace, each of these industrial giants has a unique story to tell. We explore the technological innovations, the social dynamics of the company towns that sprung up around them, and the larger-than-life personalities that shaped their destinies. Through the rise and fall of these furnaces, we witness the ebb and flow of the region's fortunes and the resilience of its people in the face of adversity.

Chapters 17 and 18 delve into the social and cultural aspects of life in the Hanging Rock Iron Region. Chapter 17 explores the development and structure of the company towns that grew up around the iron furnaces, examining how these communities shaped the lives of workers and their families. We look at the unique characteristics of these towns, from their layout and amenities to the social dynamics that governed daily life.

Chapter 18 provides a detailed look at the daily routines and challenges faced by the residents of these company towns. We explore the arduous tasks of water retrieval, soap making, and maintaining cleanliness in a world dominated by iron dust and coal soot. The chapter also examines the roles of men, women, and children in these communities, painting a vivid picture of life in the shadow of the iron furnaces.

These chapters offer a human-centered perspective on the industrial history of the region, reminding us that behind every ton of iron produced were the lives, hopes, and struggles of real people. By examining these aspects of daily life, we gain a deeper understanding of the true cost and impact of the iron industry on the communities it created.

As we reach the end of our journey, we cannot help but marvel at the incredible story of the Hanging Rock Iron Region—a story of natural bounty and human ingenuity, of ancient mysteries and industrial might. Through the pages of "Forged in Fire," we have traveled through time and space, from the primordial forces that shaped the land to the modern-day efforts to preserve and interpret its legacy. In the end, the Hanging Rock Iron Region stands as a microcosm of the American experience—a land where the dreams and struggles of countless individuals have converged to create something greater than the sum of its parts. It is a reminder of the enduring human spirit, the power of innovation and perseverance, and the deep connections that bind us to the land and to each other.

As you embark on this journey through the pages of "Forged in Fire," prepare to be captivated, enlightened, and inspired. The story of the Hanging Rock Iron Region is one that deserves to be told, and in the telling, it has the power to transform our understanding of the past, the present, and the future. So sit back, relax, and let the fires of history forge a new understanding of this remarkable land and its people.

Chapter 1

Bedrock and Bounty: The Geological Foundations of the Hanging Rock Iron Region

The Geography and Geological Foundations of the Hanging Rock Iron Region With A Bit Of Geological History.

Formation of the Appalachian Mountains

The Appalachian Mountains, often referred to as the backbone of the Eastern United States, are a geological marvel that dates back over 480 million years. These mountains were formed through a series of tectonic events known as orogenies. The first of these, the Taconic orogeny, occurred during the Ordovician period when the ancient Iapetus Ocean began to close, causing the continental plates to collide. This event marked the beginning of the Appalachian mountain-building process.

Subsequent orogenies, including the Acadian and Alleghenian orogenies, further uplifted and deformed the Appalachians, creating a range that once rivaled the Himalayas in height. The Alleghenian orogeny, occurring about 300 million years ago, was the most significant, as it resulted from the collision of the North American and African plates. This collision not only created the Appalachian range but also laid the groundwork for the formation of vast mineral deposits, including coal and iron, that would later be exploited during the Industrial Revolution.

Over millions of years, the towering peaks of the Appalachians have been weathered and eroded into the more modest mountains we see today. The region's landscape is characterized by rolling hills, deep valleys, and plateaus, each feature telling a story of ancient geological processes. The range extends from Canada down to Alabama, with the Hanging Rock Iron Region nestled within the northern reaches of the range, particularly in Ohio, Kentucky, and parts of West Virginia.

The geology of the Appalachian region is complex, with layers of sedimentary rock formed during different geological periods. The region's bedrock includes limestone, sandstone, shale, and coal beds, interspersed with rich veins of iron ore. The diversity of rock types has resulted in a variety of soil types and ecosystems, contributing to the region's rich biodiversity. Rivers and streams, including the Ohio River, have carved through the bedrock, creating steep bluffs and gorges that add to the region's dramatic landscape.

Coal Formation and Distribution

Coal formation in the Hanging Rock Iron Region is a testament to the region's ancient past, dating back to the Carboniferous period, approximately 300 million years ago. During this time, the area was part of a vast, warm, and humid environment, dominated by extensive swamps and dense forests of ferns, horsetails, and massive tree-like plants known as lycophytes.

As these plants lived and died, they accumulated in the swampy waters, creating thick layers of plant material known as peat. This peat was buried under layers of sediment over millions of years, subjected to increasing pressure and heat. This process, called coalification, gradually transformed the peat into lignite, then into bituminous coal, and in some cases, into anthracite.

The Hanging Rock Iron Region is particularly known for its deposits of bituminous coal, which is a higher grade of coal due to its higher carbon content and energy density. Bituminous coal was essential in the production of coke, a nearly pure form of carbon that burns at a high temperature and was crucial for the smelting of iron ore.

The presence of extensive coal seams in the region led to the development of a robust coal mining industry, which became a cornerstone of the local economy. Mines were established across the region, with towns and communities growing up around them. These mining operations employed thousands of workers, many of whom lived in company towns that provided housing, stores, and other amenities but were often controlled by the mining companies, leading to a unique social dynamic.

The geology of the coal deposits varies across the region, with some seams being thick and extensive, while others are thinner and more challenging to mine. The coal is found in layers, or seams, that can range from a few inches to several feet thick. Mining methods have evolved over time, from early surface mining and rudimentary underground mining to more advanced methods such as longwall mining and mountaintop removal. Each method has had a profound impact on the landscape and the people who worked in the mines.

The economic impact of coal mining in the Hanging Rock Iron Region cannot be overstated. Coal powered the furnaces that produced iron and steel, which were essential for the industrialization of the United States.

The region's coal also found markets beyond the immediate area, transported by rail and river to cities and industries across the country. The coal beds of the region are not just geological features; they are historical records of the Earth's distant past, preserving the remains of ancient forests that once thrived in a prehistoric world. These coal beds have shaped the history, economy, and culture of the Hanging Rock Iron Region, leaving an indelible mark on its landscape and its people.

The process of coalification itself is fascinating, as it represents one of nature's most efficient methods of energy storage. The energy stored in coal is essentially ancient sunlight, captured by plants millions of years ago and locked away in the Earth's crust. This stored energy has fueled human progress for centuries, from the steam engines of the Industrial Revolution to the power plants of the modern era. However, the extraction of this energy has come at a cost. The coal mines of the Hanging Rock Iron Region have altered the landscape, sometimes in dramatic ways. Entire mountains have been removed to access coal seams, valleys have been filled with the waste material, and rivers have been polluted by runoff from mining operations. The social and environmental consequences of coal mining are complex and far-reaching, shaping not only the physical landscape but also the lives of the people who call this region home.

Iron Ore Deposits

Iron ore is another critical resource found in abundance in the Hanging Rock Iron Region. The primary types of iron ore mined in the region are hematite and limonite. These ores were formed during the Silurian and Devonian periods, when the region was covered by shallow seas. As iron dissolved in the seawater, it precipitated out and settled on the sea floor, forming iron-rich sediments.

Hematite, the most common type of iron ore in the region, is a reddish-brown mineral composed of iron(III) oxide. It has a high iron content, typically around 70%, making it highly desirable for iron production. Limonite, on the other hand, is a brownish-yellow ore that contains iron in a hydrated form, often found in bogs and wetlands. While not as rich in iron content as hematite, limonite was still a valuable resource, especially in areas where hematite was less abundant.

The discovery of these iron ore deposits in the early 19th century led to a rush of industrial activity in the Hanging Rock Iron Region. Entrepreneurs and industrialists recognized the potential for iron production, given the proximity of both iron ore and coal resources. Iron furnaces began to spring up throughout the region, the most notable being the Buckeye Furnace and Vesuvius Furnace.

The process of turning iron ore into usable iron involved several steps. The ore was first mined and then transported to a furnace, where it was heated to high temperatures in the presence of coke, derived from the region's abundant coal. This process, known as smelting, caused the iron to separate from impurities in the ore, producing a molten metal that could be cast into pig iron or further refined into wrought iron or steel.

The iron produced in the Hanging Rock Iron Region was used to manufacture a wide range of products, including tools, machinery, and weapons. During the 19th century, the region became a key supplier of iron for the burgeoning American industrial economy. The iron industry also had a significant social impact, providing employment for thousands of workers and contributing to the growth of towns and communities in the region. However, the iron industry was not without its challenges. The quality and accessibility of iron ore varied across the region, and the industry was highly dependent on fluctuating market prices and technological advancements. As new iron sources were discovered in other parts of the country and new production methods were developed, the importance of the Hanging Rock Iron Region's iron industry began to wane.

Despite these challenges, the legacy of the iron industry remains an integral part of the region's history and identity.

The iron ore deposits of the Hanging Rock Iron Region are more than just geological resources; they are a testament to the complex interplay of Earth's processes over millions of years. The formation of these deposits required specific conditions, including the presence of iron-rich source rocks, the right chemical environment for iron to be dissolved and transported, and the appropriate depositional setting for the iron to accumulate and form ore bodies.

The weathering and erosion of these iron ore deposits have also played a role in shaping the region's landscape. The distinctive red and yellow hues of the soil in many parts of the region are a direct result of the presence of iron oxides, derived from the weathering of iron-rich rocks. These soils have influenced the region's ecology, supporting unique plant communities adapted to the high iron content.

The human history of the Hanging Rock Iron Region is inextricably linked to these iron ore deposits. The rise of the iron industry in the 19th century transformed the region, bringing economic growth, technological innovation, and social change. The legacy of this industry can still be seen in the region's towns and cities, many of which grew up around the iron furnaces and mines that once drove the local economy.

Today, the iron ore deposits of the Hanging Rock Iron Region are no longer actively mined, but their influence on the region's history and identity remains profound. The story of these deposits is a reminder of the complex interplay between geology, ecology, and human activity that has shaped this unique landscape over millions of years.

Chemical Composition and Geological Formations

The geological formations of the Hanging Rock Iron Region are not only significant for their historical impact on industry but also for their rich chemical compositions. These compositions played a critical role in determining the types of resources available and their suitability for industrial use.

Limestone, a key component of the region's bedrock, is primarily composed of calcium carbonate ($CaCO_3$). This sedimentary rock is formed from the skeletal fragments of marine organisms such as coral and mollusks. The presence of limestone in the region contributed to the soil's alkalinity, which in turn affected the types of vegetation that could thrive there. Limestone was also used as a flux in the smelting of iron ore, helping to remove impurities from the molten metal.

Sandstone, another prevalent rock type in the region, consists mainly of quartz (SiO_2) and feldspar. Sandstone's durability made it a common building material, and its porosity allowed it to serve as a reservoir for groundwater. In some parts of the Hanging Rock Iron Region, the sandstone is rich in iron oxide, giving it a reddish hue and indicating the presence of iron deposits. Shale, a fine-grained sedimentary rock, is abundant in the region and is composed of clay minerals and tiny fragments of other minerals such as quartz and calcite. Shale often contains organic material that, under the right conditions, can transform into oil and natural gas. The organic-rich shales of the region have been a source of hydrocarbons, although not as extensively exploited as coal.

Coal, as previously discussed, is a carbon-rich sedimentary rock that forms from the remains of ancient vegetation. The quality of coal varies depending on its carbon content, with anthracite being the highest grade, followed by bituminous coal, sub-bituminous coal, and lignite. The coal seams in the Hanging Rock Iron Region are predominantly bituminous, with a high carbon content that makes them particularly valuable for energy production and coke manufacturing.

Iron ores such as hematite and limonite are iron-rich minerals that were crucial to the region's iron industry. Hematite (Fe_2O_3) is composed of iron and oxygen and is known for its reddish color and high iron content. Limonite, on the other hand, is a hydrated iron oxide with a varying composition, often expressed as $FeO(OH) \cdot nH_2O$. The presence of these ores in the region provided the raw materials needed for iron production, which in turn fueled the growth of the local economy.

In addition to these major rock types, the region also contains deposits of clay, gypsum, and other minerals that have been used in various industrial applications. Clay, for example, has been used in brick-making, pottery, and as a drilling mud in oil exploration. Gypsum, a sulfate mineral composed of calcium sulfate dihydrate ($CaSO_4 \cdot 2H_2O$), has been used in the production of plaster and drywall.

The chemical composition of these geological formations not only shaped the natural landscape but also determined the economic development of the Hanging Rock Iron Region. The availability of these resources, combined with the ingenuity of the people who settled the area, led to the establishment of industries that have left a lasting legacy on the region.

The dense smoke from iron furnaces and coal-fired power plants often hung over towns and cities, creating a phenomenon known as industrial smog. In the early days of industrialization, there was little awareness of the health impacts of air pollution, and it was often seen as an inevitable consequence of progress. However, as respiratory illnesses and other health problems became more prevalent, the need for air quality improvements became increasingly apparent.

The legacy of the region's industrial activities is not solely negative, however. The development of the coal and iron industries brought economic growth and employment to the region, helping to build communities and improve the standard of living for many residents. The infrastructure established during the industrial boom, including railroads, roads, and buildings, has continued to benefit the region even as the industries themselves have declined. Efforts to mitigate the environmental impact of past industrial activities have been ongoing. Reclamation projects have sought to restore former mining sites to their natural state, reforesting areas that were once stripped bare and cleaning up polluted waterways. These efforts have met with varying degrees of success, and the long-term health of the region's ecosystems remains a topic of concern for residents and environmentalists alike.

Today, the Hanging Rock Iron Region is a place where the remnants of its industrial past coexist with efforts to preserve and protect the natural environment. The challenges faced by the region are emblematic of the broader struggles of former industrial areas across the United States, as they seek to balance economic development with environmental sustainability.

Cultural and Social Legacy

The cultural and social legacy of the Hanging Rock Iron Region is deeply intertwined with its industrial history. The coal mines, iron furnaces, and railroads that once dominated the region's economy also shaped its cultural identity and social fabric.

The influx of workers from various backgrounds to the region's mines and industrial centers brought with them a rich tapestry of cultural traditions, languages, and practices. These workers, many of whom were immigrants or descendants of immigrants, contributed to the development of a unique regional culture that blended elements of Appalachian, European, and African American traditions. This cultural diversity is reflected in the region's music, food, festivals, and religious practices, which continue to thrive today.

Labor unions played a significant role in the social history of the region, as workers organized to fight for better wages, working conditions, and safety standards. The struggles of miners and industrial workers to secure their rights were often met with resistance from employers and government authorities, leading to labor strikes, protests, and, in some cases, violent confrontations. These struggles left a lasting legacy of solidarity and collective action that continues to influence the region's social and political landscape.

The decline of the coal and iron industries in the 20th century brought significant social and economic challenges to the region. As mines and furnaces closed, many workers found themselves out of work, leading to a period of economic hardship and population decline. The loss of these industries also had a profound impact on the cultural identity of the region, as communities that had been built around mining and industrial work sought to redefine themselves in the face of a changing economic landscape.

Despite these challenges, the people of the Hanging Rock Iron Region have shown remarkable resilience and adaptability. The region has seen a resurgence of interest in its cultural heritage, with efforts to preserve historic sites, document local history, and celebrate the region's unique traditions. Cultural tourism has emerged as a new economic driver, as visitors come to explore the region's rich history, natural beauty, and vibrant communities.

The cultural and social legacy of the Hanging Rock Iron Region is a testament to the strength and perseverance of its people. Their stories, shaped by the forces of industrialization, labor struggle, and economic change, continue to resonate today, offering valuable lessons for the future.

Chapter 2

River of Progress: The Ohio's Role in Shaping the Iron Industry

The Lifeblood of Industry - The Ohio River's Role in the Hanging Rock Iron Region

As we transition from the geological foundations that shaped the Hanging Rock Iron Region, the narrative naturally flows to one of its most vital features: the Ohio River. The river's influence extends far beyond the surface, reaching deep into the economic, social, and industrial lifeblood of the region. Understanding the Ohio River's formation, exploration, and role in this area provides key insights into why the Hanging Rock Iron Region developed as it did.

Formation of the Ohio River

The Ohio River, a critical waterway in North America, has a formation history that stretches back millions of years. Its origins are deeply tied to the glacial and tectonic activities that shaped much of the continent's landscape. During the Pleistocene epoch, which began around 2.6 million years ago and lasted until about 11,700 years ago, glaciers repeatedly advanced and retreated over the region now occupied by the Ohio River. These glacial movements played a pivotal role in carving out the river's course.

As the glaciers advanced, they scoured the earth, eroding the bedrock and depositing vast amounts of sediment. When the glaciers eventually retreated, they left behind a changed landscape, with new valleys, ridges, and watercourses. The Ohio River's current path was largely determined by these glacial forces, which rerouted ancient rivers and streams into a new drainage pattern. One of the key events in the formation of the Ohio River was the melting of the Laurentide Ice Sheet, a massive glacier that covered much of North America. As this ice sheet melted, it released enormous volumes of water, which flowed into existing river valleys and helped to establish the Ohio River's course.

The river's headwaters are located in the Allegheny Plateau, where the Allegheny and Monongahela rivers converge at present-day Pittsburgh, Pennsylvania. From there, the Ohio River flows westward, traversing the Appalachian Mountains and the interior plains before joining the Mississippi River at Cairo, Illinois. Along its journey, the Ohio River passes through or borders six states: Pennsylvania, Ohio, West Virginia, Kentucky, Indiana, and Illinois.

The Ohio River basin, which encompasses over 200,000 square miles, is a major hydrological feature of the eastern United States. The basin includes numerous tributaries, such as the Kanawha, Tennessee, Cumberland, and Wabash rivers, which contribute to the Ohio River's flow and its role as a vital waterway. The river's gradual slope and relatively gentle flow made it an ideal natural highway, facilitating the movement of people and goods long before the advent of modern transportation networks.

Exploration of the Ohio River

The exploration of the Ohio River by European settlers and explorers was driven by a desire to understand and exploit the natural resources of the region. The river was seen as both a gateway and a barrier, offering opportunities for trade and expansion while also presenting challenges in the form of difficult navigation and resistance from indigenous peoples.

René-Robert Cavelier, Sieur de La Salle's 1669 expedition marked the beginning of European involvement in the Ohio River Valley. La Salle, a French explorer, was motivated by the prospects of fur trade and the expansion of French influence in the interior of North America. La Salle's journey down the Ohio River was fraught with challenges, including difficult terrain, hostile encounters with Native American tribes, and the logistical difficulties of navigating an unfamiliar and often treacherous river. Despite these obstacles, La Salle's expedition provided valuable information about the river and its potential for trade and settlement.

Following La Salle's exploration, the French sought to establish a strong presence in the Ohio River Valley to secure control over the fur trade and counter British influence in the region. They built a series of forts along the river, the most famous of which was Fort Duquesne, located at the confluence of the Allegheny and Monongahela rivers. Fort Duquesne, constructed in 1754, became a flashpoint in the struggle between France and Britain for control of the Ohio River Valley. The fort's strategic location made it a key asset for whoever controlled it, and it played a central role in the early stages of the French and Indian War.

The British, recognizing the importance of the Ohio River, were determined to challenge French dominance in the region. The Ohio Company of Virginia, a British land speculation company, was granted land in the Ohio Valley with the aim of encouraging British settlement and asserting British claims to the territory. To this end, the Ohio Company employed surveyors like Christopher Gist to explore and map the region. Gist's explorations in the early 1750s provided detailed descriptions of the Ohio River and its surrounding lands, offering valuable insights into the region's potential for agriculture and trade.

Gist's work laid the groundwork for British expansion into the Ohio River Valley, but it also heightened tensions with the French and their Native American allies. These tensions ultimately led to the outbreak of the French and Indian War, a conflict that would have profound consequences for the future of North America. The war saw numerous battles fought along the Ohio River, including the Battle of Fort Duquesne, which resulted in the fort's capture by the British and its renaming as Fort Pitt. The British victory in the war secured their control over the Ohio River Valley, paving the way for further exploration and settlement.

As the United States gained independence and expanded westward, the Ohio River continued to play a crucial role in the nation's development. The river became known as the "Gateway to the West," serving as a primary route for settlers moving into the Ohio Valley and beyond. The river's importance as a transportation corridor grew with the advent of steamboats in the early 19th century, which revolutionized travel and trade on the river. Steamboats allowed for faster and more reliable movement of goods and people, linking the Ohio River to the broader economic networks of the United States.

The exploration of the Ohio River Valley had a profound impact on the indigenous peoples who had lived in the region for centuries. As European and American settlers moved into the area, they displaced Native American communities, leading to conflicts and the eventual removal of many tribes from their ancestral lands. The Ohio River, once a vital resource for Native American cultures, became a symbol of the dramatic changes brought about by European colonization and American expansion. The river's exploration is a story of discovery and opportunity, but also of conflict and loss, reflecting the complex history of the region.

The Ohio River's exploration continued into the late 18th and early 19th centuries, as the United States gained independence and expanded westward. Pioneers and settlers used the Ohio River as a gateway to the western frontier, navigating its waters to reach the fertile lands of the Ohio Valley and beyond. The river became known as the "Gateway to the West," and its role in American expansion cannot be overstated.

The Ohio River's geological significance extends far beyond its role as a transportation route. The river itself is a product of ancient geological forces, and its formation is deeply intertwined with the history of the Earth's surface. The Ohio River is part of the larger Mississippi River system, which drains a significant portion of North America. This river system is one of the most extensive in the world, and the Ohio River is a crucial component of its eastern drainage basin.

The river's journey from its headwaters in the Allegheny Plateau to its confluence with the Mississippi River covers a diverse range of landscapes. The upper reaches of the river, where the Allegheny and

Monongahela rivers merge, are characterized by rugged terrain and steep valleys. These areas were shaped by the same glacial and tectonic forces that influenced the entire Appalachian region. As the river flows westward, it enters a broader valley, where the landscape begins to flatten out, reflecting the transition from the Appalachian Mountains to the interior plains.

The Ohio River's middle course, which runs through the Hanging Rock Iron Region, is particularly notable for its wide floodplains and fertile soils. These floodplains were formed by the river's natural meandering over thousands of years, as it deposited sediment and carved out new channels. The sediment carried by the river is a mix of materials eroded from the surrounding highlands, including clay, silt, sand, and gravel. This sediment has contributed to the development of rich agricultural lands along the river's banks, which have supported human settlement and farming for millennia.

As the Ohio River approaches its confluence with the Mississippi River, the landscape becomes even flatter and more expansive. The river's floodplain in this region is one of the most extensive in North America, covering thousands of square miles. This floodplain is a dynamic environment, shaped by regular flooding events that replenish the soil with fresh sediment. The river's periodic flooding has historically been both a blessing and a curse for the people living along its banks, providing fertile land for agriculture but also posing a constant threat to settlements and infrastructure.

The Ohio River's tributaries, including the Tennessee and Cumberland rivers, play a significant role in the river's hydrology. These tributaries drain large areas of the Appalachian Mountains and the interior plains, contributing to the Ohio River's flow and sediment load. The interaction between the Ohio River and its tributaries has created a complex network of waterways that have shaped the region's landscape and ecology. The Tennessee River, for example, drains much of the southern Appalachian region, while the Cumberland River flows through the heart of Kentucky. These tributaries not only feed the Ohio River but also create their own distinct valleys and floodplains, each with its own unique geological and ecological characteristics.

The Ohio River's role in shaping the region's landscape cannot be overstated. The river has carved out valleys, deposited fertile soils, and created wetlands that support a diverse array of plant and animal life. These natural features have provided the foundation for human settlement and industry in the region, making the Ohio River a vital part of the region's history and development. Understanding the river's geological history is key to appreciating its importance to the Hanging Rock Iron Region and the broader Appalachian region.

The exploration of the Ohio River by European powers was driven by the river's strategic importance as a transportation route and its potential for economic exploitation. The river was seen as a gateway to the interior of North America, offering access to vast tracts of land rich in natural resources. The French, who were among the first Europeans to explore the river, sought to establish a network of trade routes that would link their territories in Canada with the Mississippi River and the Gulf of Mexico. The Ohio River was a key component of this network, providing a direct route from the Great Lakes to the Mississippi River.

The French were not the only European power interested in the Ohio River. The British also recognized the river's strategic importance, and they sought to challenge French control of the region. The Ohio Company of Virginia, a British land speculation company, was granted large tracts of land in the Ohio Valley, with the goal of encouraging British settlement and establishing British dominance in the region. This competition between the French and the British eventually led to the outbreak of the French and Indian War, a conflict that would have far-reaching consequences for the future of North America.

The French and Indian War, also known as the Seven Years' War, was a global conflict that pitted France and its Native American allies against Britain and its colonial forces. The war was fought on multiple fronts, including the Ohio River Valley, where both sides sought to control key forts and trading posts. The conflict in the Ohio River Valley was marked by a series of battles and skirmishes, including the Battle of Fort Necessity and the Battle of Fort Duquesne. The war ended with the Treaty of Paris in 1763, which saw France cede control of its territories in North America to Britain.

The British victory in the French and Indian War secured their control over the Ohio River Valley, but it also set the stage for further conflicts. The Proclamation of 1763, issued by King George III, sought to prevent further colonial expansion into Native American territories by establishing a boundary along the Appalachian Mountains. This proclamation angered many British colonists, who saw it as an infringement on their rights to settle and exploit the lands west of the Appalachians. The tensions between the British government and its colonial subjects would eventually lead to the American Revolution.

During the American Revolution, the Ohio River played a significant role in the conflict between the American colonies and the British Empire. The river served as a boundary between British-controlled territories to the north and the American frontier to the south. Both sides sought to control the river and its surrounding lands, leading to a series of military campaigns and skirmishes in the Ohio River Valley.

The river's strategic importance was underscored by its role as a transportation route for troops, supplies, and communication between the eastern seaboard and the western frontier.

After the American Revolution, the Ohio River became a vital artery for the westward expansion of the United States. The river was the primary route for pioneers and settlers moving into the Ohio Valley and beyond, earning it the nickname "Gateway to the West." The river's role in American expansion was further solidified by the construction of forts, trading posts, and settlements along its banks. The river also became a crucial transportation route for the growing American economy, as goods produced in the interior of the country were transported down the river to markets in the east and abroad.

The development of steamboat technology in the early 19th century revolutionized travel and trade on the Ohio River. Steamboats allowed for faster and more reliable transportation of goods and people, transforming the river into a bustling commercial highway. The Ohio River became the lifeblood of the growing American economy, linking the agricultural heartlands of the Midwest with the industrial centers of the Northeast and the markets of the Gulf Coast. The river's importance to the development of the United States cannot be overstated, as it played a key role in the country's westward expansion and economic growth.

Chapter 3

From Earth to Furnace: The Journey of Iron Ore in Hanging Rock

Basic Analysis of Ore Acquisition and Transportation in the Hanging Rock Iron Region

Acquisition of Iron Ore

Locations and Discovery of Ore Deposits

The Hanging Rock Iron Region, which includes southern Ohio, northeastern Kentucky, and western West Virginia, was rich in iron ore deposits, particularly hematite (Fe_2O_3) and magnetite (Fe_3O_4). Specific areas of significant iron ore deposits include Lawrence and Scioto counties in Ohio, Greenup and Carter counties in Kentucky, and parts of the Appalachian Plateau in West Virginia. The geological formations in these regions, such as iron-rich sandstone and shale, indicated the presence of iron ore, and early settlers often discovered these deposits through natural outcrops.

Depth and Extent of Ore Deposits

The depth of iron ore deposits in the Hanging Rock Iron Region varied considerably. Surface deposits were sometimes found just a few feet below the ground surface, particularly in hilly areas where erosion had exposed the iron-rich layers. However, many deposits required deeper mining operations, with veins extending over a hundred feet underground. Miners would often dig test pits to assess the depth and richness of the ore before deciding on full-scale extraction. The ore's depth influenced the choice of mining methods, whether surface mining or more complex underground mining techniques.

Varieties of Iron Ore

The Hanging Rock region primarily yielded two types of iron ore: hematite (Fe_2O_3) and magnetite (Fe_3O_4). Hematite, a reddish-brown ore, was the most common and preferred due to its high iron content and ease of reduction in blast furnaces. Magnetite, although less abundant, was also mined and used in iron production. Additionally, some areas contained limonite ($FeO(OH) \cdot nH_2O$), a hydrous iron oxide ore that was often found in bogs and low-lying areas. Each type of ore required different processing techniques, which were developed to optimize iron yield.

Mining Methods and Extraction

Iron ore extraction in the Hanging Rock region employed both surface and underground mining methods. Surface mining, including open-pit mining, was used where ore was near the surface. Miners removed the overburden (soil and rock) using hand tools such as picks and shovels, or later, blasting techniques. The exposed ore was broken down manually or with mechanical tools before being transported to the surface.

In areas where the ore was located deeper underground, more complex methods were required. Shaft mining involved digging vertical shafts to reach the ore veins, while drift mining involved horizontal tunnels following the ore veins. These mines required significant manpower and often dangerous working conditions. The ore was extracted by drilling and blasting, then loaded into carts and transported to the surface using pulley systems or other lifting mechanisms.

Transportation of Iron Ore to the Furnaces

Early Transport Methods

Once the ore was extracted, it needed to be transported to the iron furnaces, which were often located miles away from the mining sites. In the early years, transportation was primarily achieved through oxen and horse-drawn carts. These carts carried the ore over rough, unpaved roads. The journey was slow, especially over hilly or uneven terrain, and the quantity of ore that could be moved was limited. Transporting ore overland in this manner was labor-intensive and time-consuming, and the condition of the roads often dictated the pace of the iron production process.

Development of Canals and Railroads

As the iron industry in the Hanging Rock region expanded, the need for more efficient transportation methods became apparent. The construction of canals, particularly the Ohio and Erie Canal, provided a water-based transport system that significantly increased the volume of ore that could be moved. Ore was loaded onto barges at mining sites and transported via canals to furnaces or transshipment points. This method was faster and more cost-effective than overland transport, although it was limited to areas with access to the canal network.

The advent of railroads in the mid-19th century revolutionized ore transportation in the region. Railroads provided a direct, reliable means of transporting large quantities of ore over long distances. Iron ore was loaded into railcars at the mining sites and transported to the furnaces. The construction of railroads allowed the iron industry to expand further, as ore from more remote locations could now be economically transported to the furnaces. Rail transport also reduced the time required to move ore, increasing the efficiency of the overall production process.

Innovations in Transportation Methods

Throughout the 19th century, several innovations improved the transportation of iron ore. The development of steam-powered locomotives allowed for the hauling of heavier loads, while the construction of dedicated railway lines to the furnaces ensured a steady supply of ore. Additionally, improvements in road construction and the use of larger, more durable carts allowed for increased overland transport when rail or canal access was not available.

These innovations, combined with the expanding network of canals and railroads, enabled the Hanging Rock Iron Region to sustain high levels of iron production, meeting the growing demand for iron in the United States.

The acquisition and transportation of iron ore in the Hanging Rock Iron Region were complex processes that evolved over time. From the initial discovery and extraction methods to the development of advanced transportation infrastructure, the region's ability to efficiently mine and transport iron ore was crucial to its success as a leading iron producer in the 19th century. The advancements in transportation, particularly the construction of canals and railroads, played a significant role in enabling the iron industry to thrive in this region.

Chapter 4

Amanda's Flame: The Rise and Fall of Amanda Furnace

The History and Legacy of Amanda Furnace and Its Company Town

Amanda Furnace: Comprehensive History

Amanda Furnace, established in 1829 in Lawrence County, Ohio, was one of the key iron furnaces that contributed to the industrial prominence of the Hanging Rock Iron Region during the 19th century. The furnace was named after Amanda Carpenter, a member of the influential Carpenter family who were instrumental in the development of the iron industry in Southern Ohio. Amanda Furnace played a crucial role in the production of pig iron, which was vital for the industrial growth of the United States.

Founders and Early Development

Amanda Furnace was founded by the Carpenter family, who were prominent figures in the iron industry in the Hanging Rock Iron Region. The family's involvement in the establishment of multiple furnaces in the region, including Vesuvius and Union furnaces, underscores their significant impact on the region's industrial landscape. The location of Amanda Furnace was chosen for its proximity to essential resources, including rich deposits of iron ore, abundant forests for charcoal production, and access to the nearby waterways.

The construction of Amanda Furnace was a major undertaking, requiring substantial investment and labor. The furnace was designed as a charcoal-fired blast furnace, utilizing the cold-blast method that was typical of the time. The furnace's stone stack, which housed the smelting operations, was built using locally sourced materials. The site was strategically located to ensure efficient production and transportation of pig iron to markets across the country.

Operations and Workforce

Amanda Furnace was a large-scale industrial operation that employed a significant workforce. At its peak, the furnace employed over 150 workers, including skilled furnace operators, colliers (charcoal burners), miners, blacksmiths, and general laborers. The workers were typically housed in company-owned housing near the furnace site, forming a community that was heavily reliant on the furnace for economic stability.

The production process at Amanda Furnace began with the mining of iron ore from the surrounding hills. The ore was transported to the furnace, where it was combined with charcoal and limestone in the furnace stack. The cold-blast method, while labor-intensive, produced high-quality pig iron that was in great demand for various industrial applications, including the construction of railroads, machinery, and tools.

The work at Amanda Furnace was physically demanding and required long hours, especially for those involved in charcoal production and furnace operation. The process of producing charcoal was particularly labor-intensive, involving the cutting down of trees, stacking the wood in large piles, and slowly burning it to create charcoal, which was then transported to the furnace. The furnace operated continuously, with workers maintaining the furnace around the clock to ensure a steady supply of pig iron.

Economic Impact

Amanda Furnace played a significant role in the economic development of Lawrence County and the broader Hanging Rock Iron Region. The furnace provided steady employment for hundreds of workers and supported the growth of local businesses that supplied goods and services to the furnace and its workers. The success of Amanda Furnace also attracted additional investment into the region, leading to the establishment of other iron furnaces and related industries.

The iron produced at Amanda Furnace was used in a variety of applications, including the construction of railroads, machinery, and tools, all of which were essential to the industrial growth of the United States during the 19th century. The furnace's operations also supported local agriculture, as farmers supplied food and other necessities to the growing population.

Decline and Closure

As the 19th century progressed, Amanda Furnace, like many other charcoal-fired furnaces in the region, began to face significant challenges. The depletion of local timber resources made charcoal production increasingly difficult and expensive. Additionally, the rise of coke-fired blast furnaces, which were more efficient and produced higher-quality iron, made the older charcoal furnaces less competitive.

By the late 19th century, Amanda Furnace was struggling to remain profitable. The furnace eventually ceased operations in the 1880s, marking the end of an era for Lawrence County. The closure of Amanda Furnace had a significant impact on the local community, leading to job losses and economic decline. Many of the workers who had depended on the furnace for their livelihoods were forced to leave the area in search of work elsewhere.

Legacy and Preservation

Today, the site of Amanda Furnace is recognized as a historical landmark, though little remains of the original structure. Efforts have been made to preserve what is left of the furnace and to educate the public about its historical significance. Interpretive markers at the site provide information about the history of Amanda Furnace and its role in the development of the Hanging Rock Iron Region.

The legacy of Amanda Furnace is preserved through ongoing research and documentation by local historians and preservationists. Artifacts and records related to the furnace are displayed in local museums, where they serve as a testament to the region's rich industrial heritage. The story of Amanda Furnace is a reminder of the hard work and ingenuity of the men and women who built and operated the furnace, and of the vital role that the Hanging Rock Iron Region played in the industrialization of the United States.

Modern Legacy

In addition to its historical significance, the site of Amanda Furnace is part of a broader effort to preserve the industrial heritage of the Hanging Rock Iron Region. The furnace is one of several sites in the region that have been recognized for their importance in the history of American industry. Interpretive markers and educational programs help visitors understand the role that these furnaces played in the development of the United States and the impact they had on the lives of the people who lived in this frontier.

Amanda Furnace's story is one of industrial success and decline, as well as community and resilience. The furnace helped shape the social and economic fabric of Lawrence County, leaving a lasting legacy that continues to be felt in the region today. As such, Amanda Furnace remains an important part of Southern Ohio's cultural and historical identity.

The story of Amanda Furnace would not be complete without understanding the lives of those who lived and worked in the shadow of its towering stack. The company town that grew around the furnace was as much a part of its legacy as the iron it produced. This is the story of that town.

The Company Town of Amanda Furnace: An Historical Overview

The Structure of Amanda Furnace's Company Town

The company town associated with Amanda Furnace was an essential part of the furnace's operations, providing a self-contained environment for the workers and their families. The town was situated close to the furnace to minimize travel time for the workers, and its layout reflected the needs of the community. The town included worker housing, a general store, a schoolhouse, and a church, all centered around the furnace, which was the focal point of the community.

Housing in Amanda Furnace's company town was modest and functional, consisting of small wooden structures that provided basic shelter for the workers and their families. These homes were built by the furnace company and rented to workers at a nominal fee, which was often deducted directly from their wages. The proximity of the housing to the furnace was a key feature, as it allowed workers to quickly respond to the demands of their jobs without the need for lengthy commutes.

The general store in Amanda Furnace's company town played a central role in the daily lives of the residents. Operated by the furnace company, the store stocked a range of essential goods, including food, clothing, and household items. Workers typically purchased these items on credit, with the costs deducted from their paychecks, creating an economic dependency on the company. The store was more than just a place to buy goods; it was a social hub where residents could gather, share news, and discuss social matters.

Education was provided by a small schoolhouse located within the town. The school offered basic instruction in reading, writing, and arithmetic, and it was attended by the children of the furnace workers.

Education was valued, but it was often cut short as older children were expected to contribute to the family income by working in the furnace or related industries.

The church in Amanda Furnace's company town was a vital part of the community. Supported by the furnace company, the church served as both a place of worship and a gathering spot for social events. The church played a significant role in maintaining social cohesion and promoting moral behavior within the town, and it was a key institution in the lives of the residents.

Daily Life in the Company Town

Daily life in the company town of Amanda Furnace revolved around the demanding schedule of the furnace. Workers typically began their day early in the morning, working long shifts that were physically exhausting and often dangerous. The work at the furnace exposed workers to extreme heat, hazardous materials, and the constant risk of injury, making it a challenging environment.

After their shifts, workers returned to their homes in the company town, where they spent time with their families and engaged in community activities. The general store was a central part of daily life, not only as a place to buy goods but also as a social gathering spot. The store was often the only source of goods for the residents, and its role in the community extended beyond commerce, serving as a place where people could connect and share news.

Women in the town played a crucial role in managing the household, caring for children, and often contributing to the family income through activities such as sewing, laundry, or working in the company store. The division of labor in the town was typical of the time, with men working at the furnace and women responsible for domestic tasks.

Social life in the town was centered around the church and community events, which provided opportunities for residents to come together, share news, and support each other. The church organized social events, religious services, and community gatherings, which were essential for maintaining a sense of community and solidarity among the residents.

Social Life and Community

Despite the challenges of life in the company town, the residents of Amanda Furnace developed a strong sense of community. The shared experience of working at the furnace, combined with the close-knit nature of the town, fostered a bond among residents. Social life in the town centered around the church and community events, which provided opportunities for residents to come together, share news, and support each other.

Community celebrations, such as religious holidays, picnics, and dances, were highlights of social life in the town. These events offered a welcome break from the demands of work and allowed residents to relax and enjoy each other's company. The church, as the social hub of the town, played a key role in organizing these events and fostering a sense of unity among the residents.

The general store, as mentioned earlier, was more than just a place to purchase goods. It was a gathering place where residents could socialize, discuss the day's events, and stay informed about the happenings in the community. The store's role in daily life extended beyond commerce, making it a vital part of the town's social fabric.

Challenges and Hardships

Life in Amanda Furnace's company town was not without its difficulties. The physically demanding nature of the work at the furnace, combined with the economic constraints of living in a company-owned town, placed significant stress on workers and their families. Health and safety were major concerns, as accidents and illnesses were common, and access to medical care was often limited.

The economic system of the company town, where workers were paid in company scrip that could only be used at the company store, further exacerbated the challenges faced by residents. This system created a cycle of debt and dependence, making it difficult for workers to leave the town or seek better opportunities elsewhere. The limited availability of education and other social services also meant that children were often expected to contribute to the family's income from a young age, perpetuating the cycle.

Despite these challenges, the residents of the company town showed remarkable resilience. They developed close-knit communities where mutual support and solidarity were essential for survival. Families relied on each other for assistance, whether it was sharing food, helping with childcare, or providing moral support during difficult times. The church also played a vital role in offering spiritual and emotional support, helping residents cope with the challenges of daily life.

The Decline of Amanda Furnace and Its Company Town

As the iron industry in the Hanging Rock Iron Region began to decline in the late 19th century, so too did the company town associated with Amanda Furnace. The depletion of local resources, including timber for charcoal and accessible iron ore deposits, made it increasingly difficult for the furnace to remain profitable. Additionally, the rise of more efficient coke-fired blast furnaces in other regions reduced the competitiveness of charcoal furnaces like Amanda.

The closure of Amanda Furnace had a profound impact on the company town. Without the furnace to provide employment and economic stability, many residents were forced to leave in search of work elsewhere. The company store, school, and church gradually closed, and the town's population dwindled. Buildings fell into disrepair, and the once-thriving community became a ghost town, with only a few remnants of its former life remaining.

Today, the site of Amanda Furnace's company town is largely forgotten, with few physical traces of its existence. However, the stories of the workers and their families who lived and worked in the town are an important part of the region's history. These stories serve as a reminder of the challenges and hardships faced by those who contributed to the development of the American iron industry, and of the resilience and determination that characterized life in the company towns of the Hanging Rock Iron Region.

The company town of Amanda Furnace was a microcosm of the broader iron industry in the Hanging Rock Iron Region. It was a place where the demands of industrial production shaped every aspect of daily life, from work and housing to social and community activities. While life in the company town was often challenging and fraught with hardships, it was also marked by a strong sense of community and shared purpose.

As we look back on the history of the region, it is important to remember the contributions of the workers and their families who lived in these company towns. Their lives were inextricably linked to the furnaces that fueled the growth of the nation, and their stories are an essential part of the legacy of the Hanging Rock Iron Region. The decline of the company towns, like that of the iron industry itself, was a reflection of broader economic and technological changes, but the resilience and determination of the people of the area.

Chapter 5

Iron and Earth: The Story of Buckeye Furnace and Its Community

Buckeye Furnace and Its Company Town: An Industrial Legacy

Buckeye Furnace: A Brief Historical Overview

Establishment and Early Operations

Buckeye Furnace was established in 1851 in Jackson County, Ohio, as part of the broader development of the Hanging Rock Iron Region. This region, rich in iron ore, timber, and other natural resources, became a hub for iron production during the mid-19th century. Buckeye Furnace was a cold blast charcoal furnace, which used the traditional method of smelting iron ore with charcoal made from the abundant local timber.

The furnace was designed to produce pig iron, a basic form of iron that could be further refined and used in various industrial processes. The location of Buckeye Furnace was chosen for its proximity to iron ore deposits and the availability of timber, which was essential for producing the charcoal needed for the smelting process.

Technical Details and Production

Buckeye Furnace was a typical example of the cold blast charcoal furnaces that were common in the Hanging Rock Iron Region. The furnace stack was constructed from locally sourced stone, and the interior was lined with firebrick to withstand the intense heat generated during the smelting process. The furnace was powered by a waterwheel, which drove the bellows that provided the cold air blast necessary for the smelting process.

At its peak, Buckeye Furnace could produce several tons of pig iron per day. The iron produced here was known for its high quality and was used in various applications, including the production of tools, machinery, and construction materials. The pig iron was cast into molds and allowed to cool before being transported to other locations for further processing.

Economic Impact and Workforce

The establishment of Buckeye Furnace had a significant economic impact on the surrounding area. It provided employment for a large number of workers, including laborers, craftsmen, and teamsters who transported the iron and charcoal. The furnace also supported a variety of related industries, including logging and transportation.

The workforce at Buckeye Furnace was diverse, including both local residents and immigrants who had come to the region seeking employment. The workers were typically housed in a company town adjacent to the furnace, where they had access to a company store and other basic amenities. The furnace owners often paid workers in scrip, which could only be used at the company store, creating an economic dependency on the furnace operation.

Decline and Preservation

Like many other furnaces in the Hanging Rock Iron Region, Buckeye Furnace began to decline in the late 19th century. The depletion of accessible timber for charcoal production, combined with the rise of more efficient coke-fired furnaces, made the traditional charcoal furnaces increasingly uncompetitive. By the 1890s, Buckeye Furnace had ceased operations, and the company town was gradually abandoned.

In the 20th century, efforts were made to preserve the site of Buckeye Furnace as a historical landmark. Today, Buckeye Furnace has been restored and is part of the Ohio State Parks system. The site includes a reconstructed furnace stack, a museum, and several original buildings, including the company store and workers' housing. It serves as a valuable educational resource, providing visitors with insights into the industrial history of the region.

Buckeye Furnace stands as a testament to the industrial heritage of the Hanging Rock Iron Region. Its history reflects the broader trends of 19th-century industrialization in the United States, including the rise of large-scale iron production and the development of company towns. The preservation of Buckeye Furnace allows us to appreciate the ingenuity and hard work of the people who built and operated these furnaces, and it serves as a reminder of the region's important role in the growth of America's new frontiers.

As a restored historical site, Buckeye Furnace continues to educate and inspire, offering a window into a bygone era when the production of iron was a driving force behind economic development in southern Ohio. The success and operations of Buckeye Furnace were deeply intertwined with the community that grew around it. The company town that developed adjacent to the furnace was not only a place of residence but also an essential part of the industrial enterprise. This is the story of the town that supported the furnace.

The Company Town of Buckeye Furnace: A Historical Overview

The Founding and Strategic Importance of Buckeye Furnace

Buckeye Furnace, established in 1851, was one of the earliest and most significant iron furnaces in the Hanging Rock Iron Region. Its strategic location near rich deposits of iron ore and abundant timber for charcoal production made it a key player in the early industrialization of southern Ohio. The furnace's success necessitated the creation of a company town to house the large workforce required to keep the furnace running efficiently.

The town that developed around Buckeye Furnace was designed with the needs of both the workers and the furnace in mind. Unlike some of the smaller furnaces in the region, Buckeye required a larger, more organized community to support its operations. The town was laid out with a clear hierarchy, reflecting the social and economic status of its residents, from the workers who toiled in the furnace to the managers who oversaw its operations.

Distinctive Features of Buckeye Furnace's Company Town

One of the most distinctive features of Buckeye Furnace's company town was its scale. As one of the largest furnaces in the region, Buckeye required a substantial workforce, and the town that grew up around it reflected this need. The town included not only worker housing but also a range of amenities that were uncommon in smaller company towns. These included a well-equipped general store, a dedicated schoolhouse, and even a small medical clinic to care for injured or ill workers.

The housing in Buckeye Furnace's company town was also more varied than in other towns. While most workers lived in simple, functional homes, the town also featured larger, more comfortable houses for the furnace's managers and key personnel. These homes were often located on higher ground, away from the noise and smoke of the furnace, reflecting the social stratification within the town.

Another distinctive aspect of the town was its focus on education and training. Recognizing the importance of a skilled workforce, the furnace company invested in the education of both children and adults. The schoolhouse in Buckeye Furnace's company town was one of the better-equipped in the region, offering a more comprehensive curriculum than was typical for the time. In addition to basic literacy and arithmetic, the school also provided instruction in technical skills that were directly applicable to the furnace's operations.

Social Dynamics and Community Life

The social dynamics of Buckeye Furnace's company town were shaped by the shared experiences of its residents, who were bound together by the demands of their work and the isolation of their location. The town's relative remoteness meant that residents relied heavily on each other for support, creating a close-knit community where cooperation and mutual aid were essential for survival.

The communal nature of the town's layout encouraged social interaction, with the "commons" serving as a focal point for community life. Here, residents would gather to discuss the day's events, share news, and organize social activities. The town's small size and close quarters meant that everyone knew each other, and relationships were often characterized by a strong sense of solidarity and mutual respect.

Education and religion played significant roles in the social fabric of Buckeye Furnace's company town. The town's schoolhouse was not only a place of learning for the children but also a center for adult education and community gatherings. Similarly, the church provided spiritual guidance and a venue for social events, reinforcing the moral and ethical values that were important to the community.

The town's residents also participated in various forms of recreation, despite the demanding nature of their work. Sports, music, and communal meals were common, providing much-needed relief from the rigors of life at the furnace. These activities helped to strengthen the bonds between residents, making the community more resilient in the face of the challenges they encountered.

Challenges and Adaptations

Living and working in Buckeye Furnace's company town came with its share of challenges. The physical demands of the work were extreme, with long hours spent in dangerous conditions. The heat, noise, and risk of injury were constant companions for the workers, who had to remain vigilant at all times to avoid accidents. Despite these dangers, the work was steady, and the residents of the town took pride in their contributions to the furnace's success.

Economic fluctuations in the iron industry also posed challenges for the town's residents. Periods of high demand were often followed by downturns, during which wages might be reduced or work might be scarce. The town's reliance on the furnace for its economic stability meant that these fluctuations had a direct impact on the livelihoods of its residents.

In response to these challenges, the community of Buckeye Furnace's company town developed a number of strategies for coping and adaptation. The emphasis on communal spaces and mutual support helped to buffer the impact of economic and social stressors.

Additionally, the town's residents were resourceful, often finding ways to supplement their incomes through side projects, such as small-scale farming, crafting, or trading goods with neighboring communities.

The Decline and Legacy of Buckeye Furnace's Company Town

The decline of Buckeye Furnace began in the late 19th century, as the iron industry in the Hanging Rock Iron Region faced increased competition and technological changes. The advent of more efficient production methods, coupled with the depletion of local resources, made it difficult for the furnace to remain viable. By the 1890s, the economic pressures had become too great, leading to the eventual closure of the furnace.

With the closure of Buckeye Furnace, the company town gradually declined as well. The population dwindled as residents left in search of work elsewhere, and the once-vibrant community began to fade. The homes, once filled with the sounds of daily life, fell silent, and the communal spaces that had been the heart of the town were abandoned.

Today, Buckeye Furnace has been preserved as a historical site, offering visitors a glimpse into the life of an iron furnace town in the 19th century. The preserved furnace and reconstructed buildings serve as a testament to the resilience and ingenuity of the people who lived and worked there. The legacy of Buckeye Furnace's company town is one of hard work, community spirit, and adaptation in the face of changing economic realities.

Buckeye Furnace's company town was a significant part of the iron industry in the Hanging Rock Iron Region. Its size, diversity, and emphasis on education and community made it a distinctive example of a company town, offering insights into the social and economic dynamics of the time. While the town ultimately declined along with the furnace, its legacy continues to be felt in the history of the region.

As we reflect on the history of Buckeye Furnace's company town, it is important to recognize the contributions of its residents to the growth of the iron industry and to the development of community life in industrial America. Their experiences offer valuable lessons about the challenges and opportunities of industrialization, and they remind us of the human stories that are at the heart of our industrial heritage.

Chapter 6

The Cambria Chronicles: The Birth and Legacy of an Iron Town

Cambria Furnace and Its Company Town: An Industrial Legacy

In-Depth History of the Iron Furnaces in the Hanging Rock Iron Region

Cambria Furnace

Location: Jackson County, Ohio Founded: 1854 Founder(s): Peter B. Calder and John Campbell. Cambria Furnace, founded in 1854 by Peter B. Calder and John Campbell, was one of the last major furnaces established in the Hanging Rock Iron Region. Located in Jackson County, Ohio, Cambria Furnace was notable for its adoption of new technologies and production methods that set it apart from earlier furnaces in the region.

Operations and Workforce

Cambria Furnace employed the hot blast technique, which was a significant advancement over the cold blast method used by earlier furnaces. This technique involved preheating the air before it was introduced into the furnace, resulting in more efficient smelting and higher output. The furnace produced high-quality pig iron, which was used in various industries, including the burgeoning railroad industry.

The furnace employed around 250 workers, including furnace operators, blacksmiths, and laborers. The workforce was a mix of skilled and unskilled labor, with many workers coming from nearby communities. The furnace also contributed to the local economy by creating demand for ancillary services, such as transportation, food, and housing. Cambria Furnace played a significant role in the economic development of Jackson County, helping to establish the region as a center for iron production.

Decline and Closure

Cambria Furnace continued to operate into the late 19th century, but like many other furnaces in the region, it eventually succumbed to the pressures of resource depletion and competition from newer, more efficient production methods. The rise of the steel industry and the shift towards larger, more centralized production facilities made small, independent furnaces like Cambria less viable. The furnace ceased operations in the early 1900s, marking the end of iron production in Jackson County.

Modern Legacy

Today, the site of Cambria Furnace is recognized as a historical landmark. While much of the original structure has been lost to time, efforts to preserve the site's history continue. Local historians and preservationists work to ensure that the legacy of Cambria Furnace and its contributions to the region's industrial heritage are not forgotten. The site remains an important part of Jackson County's history and serves as a reminder of the region's once-thriving iron industry.

The success of Cambria Furnace was closely linked to the lives of those who worked there and the community that formed around it. The company town that grew alongside the furnace played a crucial role in its operations and reflected the industrial ambitions of the era. Here's a look into the life and times of Cambria Furnace's company town.

The Company Town of Cambria Furnace: A Historical Overview

The Establishment and Industrial Ambitions of Cambria Furnace

Cambria Furnace, established in 1854, was part of the second wave of iron furnace development in the Hanging Rock Iron Region. Positioned strategically to capitalize on the rich iron ore deposits in the area, Cambria Furnace was built with the ambition of becoming a major player in the regional iron industry. The furnace's establishment came at a time of growing demand for iron, driven by the expansion of railroads and the industrialization of the Midwest.

To support its operations, a company town was developed alongside the furnace. This town was designed not just to house the workers but to create a self-sustaining community that could thrive independently of the nearby towns. The founders of Cambria Furnace envisioned a community that could withstand the economic fluctuations of the iron industry, with a focus on long-term sustainability and resilience.

Unique Features and Innovations in Cambria Furnace's Company Town

Cambria Furnace's company town was distinguished by several innovative features that set it apart from other company towns in the region. One of the most notable aspects was its infrastructure, which included a more advanced water management system. The town had a series of wells and cisterns designed to ensure a steady supply of clean water, even during dry seasons. This infrastructure was critical not only for the daily needs of the residents but also for the operation of the furnace itself.

The housing in Cambria Furnace's company town reflected a shift towards more durable and comfortable living conditions. The homes were built using a combination of local stone and timber, providing better insulation and protection from the elements than the simpler wooden structures typical of earlier company towns. The town planners also incorporated gardens and green spaces around the homes, encouraging residents to engage in small-scale agriculture to supplement their diets.

Another unique feature of the town was its emphasis on worker welfare. The company established a small health clinic staffed by a full-time doctor, an uncommon amenity in company towns of the era. This clinic provided basic medical care to workers and their families, addressing the injuries and illnesses that were common in the physically demanding environment of the furnace. The presence of the clinic reflected a growing awareness of the importance of worker health to the overall productivity of the furnace.

Social Organization and Community Life

The social organization of Cambria Furnace's company town was influenced by the furnace's management, which sought to create a well-ordered and cohesive community. The town was divided into distinct areas based on the residents' roles at the furnace, with skilled workers and managers living in more substantial homes closer to the furnace, while laborers occupied simpler homes on the outskirts of the town. This division was not just physical but also reflected the social hierarchy within the town.

Despite these divisions, there was a strong sense of community in the town, fostered by shared experiences and the challenges of life in an industrial environment. The town's church was a central institution, serving as a place of worship, a community center, and a venue for social gatherings. The church organized regular services, as well as events such as community meals, holiday celebrations, and educational lectures, helping to strengthen the bonds between residents.

Education was another priority in Cambria Furnace's company town. The town's schoolhouse offered a more comprehensive education than was typical for the time, with a curriculum that included not only basic literacy and numeracy but also subjects such as science and geography. The school also served as a community center, hosting adult education classes and community meetings, further integrating the educational system into the fabric of the town's social life.

Challenges and Resilience

Life in Cambria Furnace's company town was not without its challenges. The work at the furnace was grueling, with long hours, extreme heat, and constant exposure to dangerous conditions. Despite the presence of the health clinic, injuries and health issues were common, and the physically demanding nature of the work took a toll on the workers over time.

Economic challenges also loomed large, particularly during periods of downturn in the iron industry. The fluctuations in demand for iron, coupled with competition from newer, more efficient furnaces, often led to periods of uncertainty for the residents of the town. Wages could be cut, and layoffs were a constant threat, creating a sense of instability that affected the entire community.

However, the residents of Cambria Furnace's company town displayed remarkable resilience in the face of these challenges. The strong social networks within the town, bolstered by shared religious and educational experiences, provided a support system that helped residents cope with the difficulties of life at the furnace. The emphasis on self-sufficiency, particularly through the cultivation of gardens and the use of local resources, also helped to buffer the community against economic shocks.

The Decline and Enduring Legacy of Cambria Furnace's Company Town

The decline of Cambria Furnace began in the late 19th century, as the iron industry in the Hanging Rock Iron Region faced increasing competition from more modern production methods. The furnace struggled to remain competitive, and by the 1890s, it became clear that the economic model that had sustained the town was no longer viable. The furnace ceased operations, and without its economic engine, the town began to decline.

As residents left in search of work elsewhere, the once-thriving community began to disperse. The buildings that had once housed families and community institutions fell into disrepair, and the town was gradually abandoned. However, the legacy of Cambria Furnace's company town lives on in the history of the region. The town's emphasis on infrastructure, worker welfare, and community cohesion set it apart from other company towns of the era, making it a unique example of industrial-era planning.

Today, the site of Cambria Furnace serves as a reminder of the region's rich industrial history. While little remains of the physical structures, the stories of the people who lived and worked there continue to offer valuable insights into the social and economic dynamics of the 19th century. The town's legacy is one of resilience, innovation, and a commitment to creating a sustainable community in the face of challenging circumstances.

Cambria Furnace's company town was a product of its time, reflecting both the opportunities and challenges of life in a 19th-century industrial community. The town's innovative features, including its advanced infrastructure, emphasis on worker welfare, and commitment to education, set it apart from other company towns in the region. While the town ultimately declined along with the furnace, its legacy continues to be felt in the history of the Hanging Rock Iron Region.

As we reflect on the history of Cambria Furnace's company town, it is important to recognize the contributions of its residents to the growth of the iron industry and to the development of community life in industrial America. Their experiences offer valuable lessons about the interplay between industry, community, and resilience, and they remind us of the human stories that are at the heart of our industrial heritage.

Chapter 7

Gallia's Glow: The History of Gallia Furnace

Gallia Furnace and Its Company Town: An Industrial Legacy

Gallia Furnace: Historical Overview

Gallia Furnace, established in 1844 in Gallia County, Ohio, was one of the many iron furnaces that contributed to the industrial significance of the Hanging Rock Iron Region during the 19th century. The furnace played a pivotal role in the production of pig iron, which was vital for the industrial growth of the United States during a period of rapid economic expansion. Gallia Furnace, named after Gallia County, was a key player in the local economy and a significant employer in the region.

Founders and Early Development

Gallia Furnace was founded by a group of local investors who recognized the potential of the region's rich iron ore deposits, abundant forests for charcoal production, and proximity to transportation routes like the Ohio River. The furnace was constructed using local stone and was designed as a charcoal-fired blast furnace, utilizing the cold-blast method that was common in the region at the time.

The site for Gallia Furnace was strategically chosen to optimize access to the necessary resources. The surrounding hills provided rich deposits of iron ore, while the dense forests supplied the wood needed to produce charcoal. The furnace's location near transportation routes facilitated the movement of pig iron to markets throughout the United States.

Operations and Workforce

Gallia Furnace was a significant industrial operation that employed a substantial workforce to manage its various processes. At its peak, the furnace employed around 150 workers, including skilled furnace operators, colliers (charcoal burners), miners, and general laborers. The workers were typically housed in company-owned housing near the furnace site, forming a community that was heavily reliant on the furnace for economic stability.

The production process at Gallia Furnace involved several stages. First, iron ore was mined from the surrounding hills and transported to the furnace. The ore was then combined with charcoal and limestone in the furnace stack, where it was heated to high temperatures to extract the iron. The cold-blast method was initially used, where unheated air was blown into the furnace to aid the smelting process. This method, while labor-intensive, produced high-quality pig iron that was in great demand for various needs local and abroad.

The work at Gallia Furnace was physically demanding and required long hours, especially for those involved in charcoal production and furnace operation. The process of producing charcoal was particularly labor-intensive, involving the cutting down of trees, stacking the wood in large piles, and slowly burning it to create charcoal, which was then transported to the furnace. The furnace operated continuously, with shifts of workers maintaining the furnace around the clock to ensure a steady supply of pig iron.

Economic Impact

Gallia Furnace played a significant role in the economic development of Gallia County and the broader Hanging Rock Iron Region. The furnace provided steady employment for hundreds of workers and supported the growth of local businesses that supplied goods and services to the furnace and its workers. The success of Gallia Furnace also attracted additional investment into the region, leading to the establishment of other iron furnaces and related industries.

The iron produced at Gallia Furnace was used in a variety of applications, including the construction of railroads, machinery, and tools, all of which were essential to the industrial growth of the United States during the 19th century. The furnace's operations also supported local agriculture, as farmers supplied food and other necessities to the growing population.

Decline and Closure

As the 19th century progressed, Gallia Furnace, like many other charcoal-fired furnaces in the region, began to face significant challenges. The depletion of local timber resources made charcoal production increasingly difficult and expensive. Additionally, the rise of coke-fired blast furnaces, which were more efficient and produced higher-quality iron, made the older charcoal furnaces less competitive.

By the late 19th century, Gallia Furnace was struggling to remain profitable. The furnace eventually ceased operations in the 1880s, marking the end of an era for Gallia County. The closure of Gallia Furnace had a significant impact on the local community, leading to job losses and economic decline. Many of the workers who had depended on the furnace for their livelihoods were forced to leave the area in search of work elsewhere.

Legacy and Preservation

Today, the site of Gallia Furnace is recognized as a historical landmark, though few remnants of the original structure remain. Efforts have been made to preserve what is left of the furnace and to educate the public about its historical significance. Interpretive markers at the site provide information about the history of Gallia Furnace and its role in the development of the Hanging Rock Iron Region.

The legacy of Gallia Furnace is preserved through ongoing research and documentation by local historians and preservationists. Artifacts and records related to the furnace are displayed in local museums, where they serve as a testament to the region's rich industrial heritage. The story of Gallia Furnace is a reminder of the hard work and ingenuity of the men and women who built and operated the furnace, and of the vital role that the Hanging Rock Iron Region played in the industrialization of the United States.

Modern Legacy

In addition to its historical significance, the site of Gallia Furnace is part of a broader effort to preserve the industrial heritage of the Hanging Rock Iron Region. The furnace is one of several sites in the region that have been recognized for their importance in the history of American industry. Interpretive markers and educational programs help visitors understand the role that these furnaces played in the development of the United States and the impact they had on the lives of the people who lived in the area.

Gallia Furnace's story is one of industrial success and decline, as well as community and resilience. The furnace helped shape the social and economic fabric of Gallia County, leaving a lasting legacy that continues to be felt in the region today. As such, Gallia Furnace remains an important part of Southern Ohio's cultural and historical identity.

The operations of Gallia Furnace were supported by the company town that grew around it. This town was not just a place of residence for workers but also an essential element of the furnace's operations. Let's explore the life and community that made Gallia Furnace possible.

The Company Town of Gallia Furnace: An Historical Overview

The Development and Layout of Gallia Furnace's Company Town

Gallia Furnace was established in 1844 as part of the expanding iron industry in the Hanging Rock Iron Region. To support the operations of the furnace, a company town was developed nearby. This town was carefully planned to meet the needs of the workers and their families, with a layout that included housing, a general store, a schoolhouse, and a church, all organized around the furnace, which served as the central hub of the community.

The housing provided in Gallia Furnace's company town consisted of simple wooden cottages, built by the furnace company. These homes were basic but functional, offering essential shelter for the workers and their families. Rent for these homes was deducted directly from the workers' wages, creating a system where employment at the furnace was directly tied to housing. The close proximity of the homes to the furnace ensured that workers could easily reach their jobs, even on short notice.

The general store in Gallia Furnace's company town was a critical part of daily life. Operated by the furnace company, the store offered a variety of goods, including food, clothing, and household items. Workers typically purchased these items on credit, with the costs deducted from their paychecks. This system of company credit created an economic dependency on the furnace company, as workers often found themselves in debt to the store, making it difficult to leave or seek other opportunities.

The schoolhouse in Gallia Furnace's company town provided basic education to the children of the workers. The curriculum focused on fundamental subjects such as reading, writing, and arithmetic, preparing children for future employment in the furnace or related industries. Education was valued, but it was often cut short as older children were expected to contribute to the family income by working at the furnace.

The church in Gallia Furnace's company town played a central role in the community. It served as a place of worship and a gathering spot for social events. Supported by the furnace company, the church helped to foster a sense of community among the residents, providing spiritual guidance and emotional support in what was often a challenging and demanding environment.

Daily Life in Gallia Furnace's Company Town

Life in the company town of Gallia Furnace was closely tied to the furnace's operations. Workers typically began their day early, with long shifts that were physically demanding and often hazardous. The intense heat, noise, and the constant risk of accidents made working at the furnace a challenging occupation. Despite the challenges, the work was a source of pride for many, as the iron produced at Gallia Furnace contributed significantly to the industrial growth of the region.

After the workday, the company town provided a refuge where workers could relax and spend time with their families.

The general store was a key part of daily life, serving not just as a place to purchase goods but as a social hub where residents could catch up on local news and enjoy a sense of camaraderie. The credit system at the store, while a source of economic pressure, also fostered a sense of mutual dependency that strengthened community bonds.

Women in the company town played essential roles in maintaining households and contributing to the family income through a variety of means, including taking in boarders, sewing, and other domestic work. Their contributions were essential to the survival and well-being of their families, particularly in a setting where every member of the household was expected to contribute.

Social life in the town revolved around the church and occasional community gatherings. The church organized events such as religious services, community meals, and holiday celebrations, which were important for maintaining morale and fostering a sense of belonging among the residents. These gatherings provided a respite from the hardships of daily life and helped to build a strong community spirit.

Challenges Faced by the Residents

Living and working in Gallia Furnace's company town presented numerous challenges. The physical demands of working at the furnace were severe, with long hours, dangerous conditions, and little room for error. Injuries were common, and medical care was often inadequate, leading to long-term health problems for many workers.

The harsh working environment took a toll not just on the workers' physical health but also on their mental well-being.

Economic challenges were also significant. The system of payment in company scrip, which could only be used at the company store, meant that workers were often trapped in a cycle of debt. This economic dependency on the furnace company made it difficult for workers to leave and seek better opportunities elsewhere, effectively tying their fortunes to the success of the furnace.

The limited availability of education and other social services meant that children often had to contribute to the family's income from a young age, limiting their opportunities for advancement. This perpetuated a cycle of poverty and dependence, as children followed in their parents' footsteps, working at the furnace and living in the company town.

Despite these hardships, the residents of Gallia Furnace's company town demonstrated resilience and solidarity. The close-knit nature of the community provided a support network that was crucial for survival in such a demanding environment. Families and neighbors relied on each other for help with childcare, food, and emotional support, creating a strong sense of community in the face of adversity.

The Decline of Gallia Furnace's Company Town

As the 19th century progressed, the iron industry in the Hanging Rock Iron Region began to decline, and Gallia Furnace was no exception. The depletion of accessible iron ore deposits and the increasing difficulty of sourcing timber for charcoal production made it harder for the furnace to remain competitive. By the 1890s, the rise of coke-fired blast furnaces, which were more efficient and cost-effective, further reduced the viability of older charcoal furnaces like Gallia.

The closure of Gallia Furnace in the early 20th century had a profound impact on the company town. With the furnace no longer in operation, the town lost its primary source of employment and economic stability. Many residents were forced to leave in search of work elsewhere, leading to a gradual decline in the town's population. The general store, school, and church eventually closed, and the town's buildings fell into disrepair.

Today, little remains of Gallia Furnace's company town. The buildings have long since disappeared, and the area has largely reverted to nature. However, the stories of the workers and their families who lived and worked in the town remain an important part of the region's history. These stories are a testament to the resilience and determination of the people who built their lives around the furnace, and they serve as a reminder of the challenges and hardships faced by those who contributed to the growth of the area.

The company town of Gallia Furnace was a microcosm of the broader iron industry in the Hanging Rock Iron Region. It was a place where the demands of industrial production shaped every aspect of daily life, from work and housing to social and community activities. While life in the company town was often challenging and fraught with hardships, it was also marked by a strong sense of community and shared purpose.

As we reflect on the history of Gallia Furnace's company town, it is important to remember the contributions of the workers and their families. Their labor was essential to the growth of the iron industry and, by extension, to the industrialization of the United States. The stories of their lives offer valuable insights into the human side of industrial history and the communities that were shaped by the demands of the furnace.

Chapter 8

Huron's Heritage: The Chronicle of Huron Furnace

Huron Furnace and Its Company Town: An Industrial Legacy

Huron Furnace: Comprehensive History

Huron Furnace, established in 1855 in Lawrence County, Ohio, was one of the later iron furnaces built in the Hanging Rock Iron Region. Named after the Huron River, the furnace was part of the wave of industrial expansion that characterized the mid-19th century in Southern Ohio. Huron Furnace played a significant role in the region's iron production, contributing to the industrial growth of the United States during a critical period of economic development.

Founders and Early Development

Huron Furnace was founded by a group of investors who saw the potential in the region's abundant natural resources, including iron ore, timber for charcoal production, and access to transportation routes like the Ohio River. The furnace was constructed using local stone and was designed as a charcoal-fired blast furnace, utilizing the cold-blast method that was common in the region at the time.

The site for Huron Furnace was strategically chosen to optimize access to the necessary resources. The surrounding hills provided rich deposits of iron ore, while the dense forests supplied the wood needed to produce charcoal. The furnace's location near the Huron River allowed for efficient transportation of pig iron to markets throughout the United States.

Operations and Workforce

Huron Furnace was a large-scale industrial operation that employed a substantial workforce to manage its various processes. At its peak, the furnace employed around 150 workers, including skilled furnace operators, colliers (charcoal burners), miners, and general laborers. The workers were typically housed in company-owned housing near the furnace site, forming a community that was heavily reliant on the furnace for economic stability.

The production process at Huron Furnace involved several stages. First, iron ore was mined from the surrounding hills and transported to the furnace. The ore was then combined with charcoal and limestone in the furnace stack, where it was heated to high temperatures to extract the iron. The cold-blast method was initially used, where unheated air was blown into the furnace to aid the smelting process. This method, while labor-intensive, produced high-quality pig iron that was in great demand for various works.

The work at Huron Furnace was physically demanding and required long hours, especially for those involved in charcoal production and furnace operation. The process of producing charcoal was particularly labor-intensive, involving the cutting down of trees, stacking the wood in large piles, and slowly burning it to create charcoal, which was then transported to the furnace. The furnace operated continuously, with shifts of workers maintaining the furnace around the clock to ensure a steady supply of needed goods.

Economic Impact

Huron Furnace played a significant role in the economic development of Lawrence County and the broader Hanging Rock Iron Region. The furnace provided steady employment for hundreds of workers and supported the growth of local businesses that supplied goods and services to the furnace and its workers. The success of Huron Furnace also attracted additional investment into the region, leading to the establishment of other iron furnaces and related industries.

The iron produced at Huron Furnace was used in a variety of applications, including the construction of railroads, machinery, and tools, all of which were essential to the industrial growth of the United States during the 19th century. The furnace's operations also supported local agriculture, as farmers supplied food and other necessities to the growing population.

Decline and Closure

As the 19th century progressed, Huron Furnace, like many other charcoal-fired furnaces in the region, began to face significant challenges. The depletion of local timber resources made charcoal production increasingly difficult and expensive. Additionally, the rise of coke-fired blast furnaces, which were more efficient and produced higher-quality iron, made the older charcoal furnaces less competitive.

By the late 19th century, Huron Furnace was struggling to remain profitable. The furnace eventually ceased operations in the 1880s, marking the end of an era for Lawrence County. The closure of Huron Furnace had a significant impact on the local community, leading to job losses and economic decline. Many of the workers who had depended on the furnace for their livelihoods were forced to leave the area in search of work elsewhere.

Legacy and Preservation

Today, the site of Huron Furnace is recognized as a historical landmark, though few remnants of the original structure remain. Efforts have been made to preserve what is left of the furnace and to educate the public about its historical significance. Interpretive markers at the site provide information about the history of Huron Furnace and its role in the development of the Hanging Rock Iron Region.

The legacy of Huron Furnace is preserved through ongoing research and documentation by local historians and preservationists. Artifacts and records related to the furnace are displayed in local museums, where they serve as a testament to the region's rich industrial heritage. The story of Huron Furnace is a reminder of the hard work and ingenuity of the men and women who built and operated the furnace, and of the vital role that the Hanging Rock Iron Region played in the industrialization of the United States.

Modern Legacy

In addition to its historical significance, the site of Huron Furnace is part of a broader effort to preserve the industrial heritage of the Hanging Rock Iron Region. The furnace is one of several sites in the region that have been recognized for their importance in the history of American industry. Interpretive markers and educational programs help visitors understand the role that these furnaces played in the development of the United States and the impact they had on the lives of the people who lived in this region.

Huron Furnace's story is one of industrial success and decline, as well as community and resilience. The furnace helped shape the social and economic fabric of Lawrence County, leaving a lasting legacy that continues to be felt in the region today. As such, Huron Furnace remains an important part of Southern Ohio's cultural and historical identity.

The operations of Huron Furnace were supported by the company town that grew around it. This town was not just a place of residence for workers but also an essential element of the furnace's operations. Let's explore the life and community that made Huron Furnace possible.

The Company Town of Huron Furnace: An Historical Overview

The Structure of Huron Furnace's Company Town

The company town associated with Huron Furnace was a crucial part of the furnace's operations, providing housing and essential services to the workers and their families. Situated close to the furnace, the town's layout was designed to ensure that workers could easily access their place of employment, minimizing travel time and maintaining productivity.

Housing in Huron Furnace's company town was typical of the era, consisting of modest wooden structures that provided basic shelter for the workers and their families. These homes were constructed by the furnace company and rented to the workers at a low cost, with rent often deducted directly from their wages. The close proximity of the housing to the furnace was intentional, allowing workers to be readily available for shifts and emergencies.

The general store in Huron Furnace's company town was a central institution in the daily lives of the residents. Operated by the furnace company, the store stocked a wide range of essential goods, including food, clothing, and household items. Workers typically purchased these items on credit, with the costs deducted from their paychecks, creating an economic dependency on the company. The store was not only a place of commerce but also a social hub where residents could gather, share news, and discuss whatever.

Education was provided by a small schoolhouse located within the town. The school offered basic instruction in reading, writing, and arithmetic, primarily aimed at preparing the children of furnace workers for eventual employment in the furnace or related industries. Education was valued in the community, but it was often cut short as older children were expected to contribute to the family income.

The church in Huron Furnace's company town played a vital role in community life. Supported by the furnace company, the church served as both a place of worship and a gathering spot for social events. The church was essential in maintaining social cohesion and promoting moral behavior within the town, making it a key institution in the daily lives of the residents.

Daily Life in the Company Town

Daily life in the company town of Huron Furnace was dictated by the demanding schedule of the furnace. Workers typically began their day early in the morning, working long shifts that were physically exhausting and often hazardous. The work at the furnace exposed workers to extreme heat, toxic fumes, and the constant risk of injury, making it a challenging environment.

After their shifts, workers returned to their homes in the company town, where they spent time with their families and participated in community activities. The general store was a central part of daily life, serving as the main source of goods for the residents and a social hub where people could gather and share news. The store's role extended beyond commerce, as it was a place where residents could connect and support each other in their daily lives.

Women in the town were responsible for managing the household, caring for children, and often contributing to the family income through activities such as sewing, laundry, or even helping out in the company store. The division of labor was traditional, with men working at the furnace and women handling domestic tasks, but the women's contributions were essential to the functioning of the household and the community.

Social life in Huron Furnace's company town revolved around the church and various community events. The church organized religious services, social gatherings, and celebrations, providing residents with opportunities to come together and strengthen their sense of community. The church's influence extended into all aspects of daily life, offering spiritual guidance and emotional support to the residents.

Social Life and Community

The residents of Huron Furnace's company town developed a strong sense of community, forged through their shared experiences of working at the furnace and living in close proximity. Social life in the town was centered around the church and the general store, both of which played crucial roles in the daily lives of the residents.

Community events, such as religious holidays, picnics, and dances, were highlights of social life in the town. These events provided much-needed relief from the demands of work and allowed residents to relax and enjoy each other's company. The church, as the town's social hub, was instrumental in organizing these events and fostering a sense of unity among the residents.

The general store, beyond being a place to purchase goods, was a focal point for social interaction. It was here that residents could catch up on the latest news, share stories, and discuss the challenges they faced in their daily lives. The store's role in the community was multifaceted, making it a key part of the town's social fabric.

Challenges and Hardships

Life in Huron Furnace's company town was not without its difficulties. The physically demanding work at the furnace, combined with the economic constraints of living in a company-owned town, placed significant stress on workers and their families. Health and safety were major concerns, as accidents and illnesses were common, and access to medical care was often limited.

The economic system of the company town, where workers were paid in company scrip that could only be used at the company store, further exacerbated the challenges faced by residents. This system created a cycle of debt and dependence, making it difficult for workers to leave the town or seek better opportunities elsewhere. The limited availability of education and other social services also meant that children were often expected to contribute to the family's income from a young age, perpetuating the cycle.

Despite these challenges, the residents of the company town showed remarkable resilience. They developed close-knit communities where mutual support and solidarity were essential for survival. Families relied on each other for assistance, whether it was sharing food, helping with childcare, or providing moral support during difficult times. The church also played a vital role in offering spiritual and emotional support, helping residents cope with the challenges of daily life.

The Decline of Huron Furnace and Its Company Town

As the iron industry in the Hanging Rock Iron Region began to decline in the late 19th century, so too did the company town associated with Huron Furnace. The depletion of local resources, including timber for charcoal and accessible iron ore deposits, made it increasingly difficult for the furnace to remain profitable. Additionally, the rise of more efficient coke-fired blast furnaces in other regions reduced the competitiveness of charcoal furnaces like Huron.

The closure of Huron Furnace had a profound impact on the company town. Without the furnace to provide employment and economic stability, many residents were forced to leave in search of work elsewhere. The company store, school, and church gradually closed, and the town's population dwindled. Buildings fell into disrepair, and the once-thriving community became a ghost town, with only a few remnants of its former life remaining.

Today, the site of Huron Furnace's company town is largely forgotten, with few physical traces of its existence. However, the stories of the workers and their families who lived and worked in the town are an important part of the region's history. These stories serve as a reminder of the challenges and hardships faced by those who contributed to the development of the American iron industry, and of the resilience and determination that characterized life in the company towns of the Hanging Rock Iron Region.

The company town of Huron Furnace was a microcosm of the broader iron industry in the Hanging Rock Iron Region. It was a place where the demands of industrial production shaped every aspect of daily life, from work and housing to social and community activities. While life in the company town was often challenging and fraught with hardships, it was also marked by a strong sense of community and shared purpose.

As we look back on the history of the region, it is important to remember the contributions of the workers and their families who lived in these company towns. Their lives were inextricably linked to the furnaces that fueled the growth of the nation, and their stories are an essential part of the legacy of the Hanging Rock Iron Region. The decline of the company towns, like that of the iron industry itself, was a reflection of broader economic and technological changes, but the resilience and determination of the area.

Chapter 9

Jefferson's Journey: The Saga of Jefferson Furnace

Jefferson Furnace and Its Company Town: An Industrial Legacy

Jefferson Furnace: Available History

Jefferson Furnace, established in 1854 in Jackson County, Ohio, was one of the later iron furnaces built in the Hanging Rock Iron Region. Named in honor of President Thomas Jefferson, the furnace was part of the wave of industrial expansion that characterized the mid-19th century in Southern Ohio. Jefferson Furnace played a significant role in the production of pig iron, which was essential for the industrial growth of the United States during a critical period of economic development.

Founders and Early Development

Jefferson Furnace was founded by a group of local industrialists and investors who saw the potential in the region's abundant natural resources, including rich iron ore deposits, extensive forests for charcoal production, and access to transportation routes like the Ohio River. The furnace was constructed using locally sourced stone and was designed as a charcoal-fired blast furnace, utilizing the cold-blast method common in the region at the time.

The site for Jefferson Furnace was strategically chosen to maximize access to essential resources. The surrounding hills provided rich deposits of iron ore, while the dense forests supplied the wood needed to produce charcoal. Additionally, the furnace's location near key transportation routes facilitated the efficient movement of pig iron to markets across the United States.

Operations and Workforce

Jefferson Furnace was a large-scale industrial operation that employed a substantial workforce to manage its various processes. At its peak, the furnace employed around 150 workers, including skilled furnace operators, colliers (charcoal burners), miners, and general laborers. The workers were typically housed in company-owned housing near the furnace site, forming a close-knit community that was heavily reliant on the furnace for economic stability.

The production process at Jefferson Furnace involved several stages. First, iron ore was mined from the surrounding hills and transported to the furnace. The ore was then combined with charcoal and limestone in the furnace stack, where it was heated to high temperatures to extract the iron. The cold-blast method was initially used, where unheated air was blown into the furnace to aid the smelting process. This method, while labor-intensive, produced high-quality pig iron that was in great demand for various needs.

The work at Jefferson Furnace was physically demanding and required long hours, especially for those involved in charcoal production and furnace operation. The process of producing charcoal was particularly labor-intensive, involving the cutting down of trees, stacking the wood in large piles, and slowly burning it to create charcoal, which was then transported to the furnace. The furnace operated continuously, with shifts of workers maintaining the furnace around the clock to ensure a steady supply of purified iron.

Economic Impact

Jefferson Furnace played a significant role in the economic development of Jackson County and the broader Hanging Rock Iron Region. The furnace provided steady employment for hundreds of workers and supported the growth of local businesses that supplied goods and services to the furnace and its workers. The success of Jefferson Furnace also attracted additional investment into the region, leading to the establishment of other iron furnaces and related industries.

The iron produced at Jefferson Furnace was used in a variety of applications, including the construction of railroads, machinery, and tools, all of which were essential to the industrial growth of the United States during the 19th century. The furnace's operations also supported local agriculture, as farmers supplied food and other necessities to the growing population.

Decline and Closure

As the 19th century progressed, Jefferson Furnace, like many other charcoal-fired furnaces in the region, began to face significant challenges. The depletion of local timber resources made charcoal production increasingly difficult and expensive. Additionally, the rise of coke-fired blast furnaces, which were more efficient and produced higher-quality iron, made the older charcoal furnaces less competitive.

By the late 19th century, Jefferson Furnace was struggling to remain profitable. The furnace eventually ceased operations in the 1880s, marking the end of an era for Jackson County. The closure of Jefferson Furnace had a significant impact on the local community, leading to job losses and economic decline. Many of the workers who had depended on the furnace for their livelihoods were forced to leave the area in search of work elsewhere.

Legacy and Preservation

Today, the site of Jefferson Furnace is recognized as a historical landmark, though few remnants of the original structure remain. Efforts have been made to preserve what is left of the furnace and to educate the public about its historical significance. Interpretive markers at the site provide information about the history of Jefferson Furnace and its role in the development of the Hanging Rock Iron Region.

The legacy of Jefferson Furnace is preserved through ongoing research and documentation by local historians and preservationists. Artifacts and records related to the furnace are displayed in local museums, where they serve as a testament to the region's rich industrial heritage. The story of Jefferson Furnace is a reminder of the hard work and ingenuity of the men and women who built and operated the furnace, and of the vital role that the Hanging Rock Iron Region played in the industrialization of the area.

Modern Legacy

In addition to its historical significance, the site of Jefferson Furnace is part of a broader effort to preserve the industrial heritage of the Hanging Rock Iron Region. The furnace is one of several sites in the region that have been recognized for their importance in the history of American industry. Interpretive markers and educational programs help visitors understand the role that these furnaces played in the development of the United States and the impact they had on the lives of the people who lived here.

Jefferson Furnace's story is one of industrial success and decline, as well as community and resilience. The furnace helped shape the social and economic fabric of Jackson County, leaving a lasting legacy that continues to be felt in the region today. As such, Jefferson

Furnace remains an important part of Southern Ohio's cultural and historical identity.

The operations of Jefferson Furnace were supported by the company town that grew around it. This town was not just a place of residence for workers but also an essential element of the furnace's operations. Let's explore the life and community that made Jefferson Furnace possible.

The Company Town of Jefferson Furnace: A Historical Overview

Establishment and Historical Context

Jefferson Furnace, established in 1854, was one of the later additions to the Hanging Rock Iron Region, coming into operation during a period of significant industrial expansion in Ohio. The furnace was constructed at a time when the demand for iron was growing rapidly, fueled by the burgeoning railroad industry and the increasing need for iron infrastructure across the United States. The creation of a company town to support the furnace was a strategic decision, ensuring that the workforce was close and secured.

Unlike some of the earlier furnaces in the region, Jefferson Furnace benefited from advancements in construction techniques and industrial organization. This was reflected not only in the furnace itself but also in the design and layout of the accompanying company town. The town was laid out with a sense of order and purpose, reflecting the growing influence of industrial planning during the mid-19th century.

Unique Aspects of the Company Town

The company town associated with Jefferson Furnace was distinctive in several ways. One of its unique features was the incorporation of more durable building materials in some of the key structures, particularly the homes of the furnace managers and skilled workers. While most worker housing remained simple, these homes were constructed with better materials and often featured more elaborate designs, reflecting the status of their occupants.

Another notable aspect of Jefferson Furnace's company town was its attempt to foster a sense of community through the creation of shared spaces. Unlike earlier company towns where community life was more informally organized, Jefferson Furnace included a central meeting hall that was used for a variety of purposes, including social gatherings, educational lectures, and union meetings. This hall served as a focal point for the town, providing a space where workers could come together outside of work.

The layout of the town also included designated areas for gardening and small-scale farming, allowing residents to supplement their diets with homegrown produce. This was particularly important during periods when supply chains were disrupted, or when wages were low, providing a degree of self-sufficiency that was less common in other company towns.

Social and Cultural Life

Social and cultural life in Jefferson Furnace's company town was shaped by the diverse backgrounds of its residents. Unlike some of the earlier company towns, which were more homogeneous, Jefferson Furnace attracted workers from various parts of the United States and Europe, particularly during the 1860s when immigration to America was on the rise. This diversity brought a range of cultural practices, languages, and traditions to the town, making it a more vibrant and dynamic community.

Cultural events were common, often reflecting the traditions of the various ethnic groups within the town. These included religious festivals, traditional music and dance, and food-based celebrations that brought together the community in shared enjoyment. The central meeting hall played a significant role in hosting these events, further solidifying its place as the heart of the town's social life.

Education and literacy were also emphasized more strongly in Jefferson Furnace's company town compared to earlier settlements. The town's school was relatively well-equipped for the time, offering not only basic education but also opportunities for adults to improve their literacy and learn new skills. This focus on education was driven by the recognition that a more educated workforce could contribute to the efficiency and success of the furnace operations.

Challenges and Changes

Despite its well-planned layout and vibrant social life, Jefferson Furnace's company town was not immune to the challenges that plagued the iron industry during the late 19th century. As newer, more efficient production methods emerged and the availability of raw materials became scarcer, the furnace faced increasing difficulties in maintaining profitability. The economic downturns of the 1870s and 1880s further exacerbated these challenges, leading to periods of reduced production and layoffs.

The town's population fluctuated in response to these economic pressures, with some residents leaving to seek opportunities elsewhere, while others remained, hoping for a resurgence in the industry. The sense of community that had been carefully cultivated began to erode as economic uncertainty took its toll, and the once-thriving social life of the town became more subdued.

By the 1890s, it was clear that the heyday of Jefferson Furnace was coming to an end. The furnace ceased operations, and without its economic engine, the company town gradually declined. Many of the more durable structures survived longer than those in earlier towns, but over time, even these began to fall into disrepair as the town was abandoned.

The Legacy of Jefferson Furnace's Company Town

Today, Jefferson Furnace and its company town are remembered as part of the rich industrial history of the Hanging Rock Iron Region. While little remains of the physical structures, the stories of the people who lived and worked there continue to offer insights into the social and economic dynamics of 19th-century America. The town's emphasis on community spaces, cultural diversity, and education set it apart from other company towns of the era, making it a unique example of industrial-era planning and reformation of the ideals of workforce and the area.

The legacy of Jefferson Furnace's company town is also reflected in the descendants of those who once lived there, many of whom continue to preserve the history and traditions passed down through generations. The town's story is a reminder of the resilience of communities in the face of economic change and the importance of preserving the cultural heritage of industrial regions.

Jefferson Furnace's company town was a product of its time, shaped by the industrial demands of the mid-19th century and the social and cultural dynamics of its residents. Its unique features, including the use of more durable materials, the creation of shared community spaces, and a focus on education, set it apart from other company towns in the region. While the town ultimately declined along with the furnace, its legacy continues to be felt in the history of the Hanging Rock Iron Region and in the larger area.

As we reflect on the history of Jefferson Furnace's company town, it is important to recognize the contributions of its residents to the growth of the iron industry and to the development of community life in industrial America. Their experiences offer valuable lessons about the interplay between industry, community, and culture, and they remind us of the human stories that are at the heart of our industrial heritage.

Chapter 10

Lawrence's Labor: The Chronicle of Lawrence Furnace

Lawrence Furnace and Its Company Town: An Industrial Legacy

Lawrence Furnace: Comprehensive History

Lawrence Furnace, established in 1834 in Lawrence County, Ohio, was one of the early iron furnaces in the Hanging Rock Iron Region. Named after Lawrence County, the furnace was a significant contributor to the region's iron production during the mid-19th century. The furnace played a key role in supporting the industrialization of the United States, providing high-quality pig iron for various industries during a period of rapid economic growth.

Founders and Early Development

Lawrence Furnace was founded by a group of investors and industrialists who recognized the potential of the region's rich iron ore deposits, abundant forests for charcoal production, and access to transportation routes like the Ohio River. The furnace was constructed using local stone and was designed as a charcoal-fired blast furnace, utilizing the cold-blast method that was common in the region at the time.

The site for Lawrence Furnace was strategically chosen to optimize access to the necessary resources. The surrounding hills provided rich deposits of iron ore, while the dense forests supplied the wood needed to produce charcoal. The furnace's location near transportation routes facilitated the movement of pig iron to markets throughout the United States.

Operations and Workforce

Lawrence Furnace was a large-scale industrial operation that employed a significant workforce to manage its various processes. At its peak, the furnace employed around 150 workers, including skilled furnace operators, colliers (charcoal burners), miners, and general laborers. The workers were typically housed in company-owned housing near the furnace site, forming a community that was heavily reliant on the furnace for economic stability.

The production process at Lawrence Furnace involved several stages. First, iron ore was mined from the surrounding hills and transported to the furnace. The ore was then combined with charcoal and limestone in the furnace stack, where it was heated to high temperatures to extract the iron. The cold-blast method was initially used, where unheated air was blown into the furnace to aid the smelting process. This method, while labor-intensive, produced high-quality pig iron that was in great demand for variuos projects.

The work at Lawrence Furnace was physically demanding and required long hours, especially for those involved in charcoal production and furnace operation. The process of producing charcoal was particularly labor-intensive, involving the cutting down of trees, stacking the wood in large piles, and slowly burning it to create charcoal, which was then transported to the furnace. The furnace operated continuously, with shifts of workers maintaining the furnace around the clock to ensure a steady supply of pig iron.

Economic Impact

Lawrence Furnace played a significant role in the economic development of Lawrence County and the broader Hanging Rock Iron Region. The furnace provided steady employment for hundreds of workers and supported the growth of local businesses that supplied goods and services to the furnace and its workers. The success of Lawrence Furnace also attracted additional investment into the region, leading to the establishment of other iron furnaces and related industries.

The iron produced at Lawrence Furnace was used in a variety of applications, including the construction of railroads, machinery, and tools, all of which were essential to the industrial growth of the United States during the 19th century. The furnace's operations also supported local agriculture, as farmers supplied food and other necessities to the growing population.

Decline and Closure

As the 19th century progressed, Lawrence Furnace, like many other charcoal-fired furnaces in the region, began to face significant challenges. The depletion of local timber resources made charcoal production increasingly difficult and expensive. Additionally, the rise of coke-fired blast furnaces, which were more efficient and produced higher-quality iron, made the older charcoal furnaces less competitive.

By the late 19th century, Lawrence Furnace was struggling to remain profitable. The furnace eventually ceased operations in the 1880s, marking the end of an era for Lawrence County. The closure of Lawrence Furnace had a significant impact on the local community, leading to job losses and economic decline. Many of the workers who had depended on the furnace for their livelihoods were forced to leave the area in search of work elsewhere.

Legacy and Preservation

Today, the site of Lawrence Furnace is recognized as a historical landmark, though few remnants of the original structure remain. Efforts have been made to preserve what is left of the furnace and to educate the public about its historical significance. Interpretive markers at the site provide information about the history of Lawrence Furnace and its role in the development of the Hanging Rock Iron Region.

The legacy of Lawrence Furnace is preserved through ongoing research and documentation by local historians and preservationists. Artifacts and records related to the furnace are displayed in local museums, where they serve as a testament to the region's rich industrial heritage. The story of Lawrence Furnace is a reminder of the hard work and ingenuity of the men and women who built and operated the furnace, and of the vital role that the Hanging Rock Iron Region played in the industrialization of the United States.

Modern Legacy

In addition to its historical significance, the site of Lawrence Furnace is part of a broader effort to preserve the industrial heritage of the Hanging Rock Iron Region. The furnace is one of several sites in the region that have been recognized for their importance in the history of American industry. Interpretive markers and educational programs help visitors understand the role that these furnaces played in the development of the United States and the impact they had on the lives of the people who lived there.

Lawrence Furnace's story is one of industrial success and decline, as well as community and resilience. The furnace helped shape the social and economic fabric of Lawrence County, leaving a lasting legacy that continues to be felt in the region today. As such, Lawrence Furnace remains an important part of Southern Ohio's cultural and historical identity.

The operations of Lawrence Furnace were supported by the company town that grew around it. This town was not just a place of residence for workers but also an essential element of the furnace's operations.

Let's explore the life and community that made Lawrence Furnace possible.

The Company Town of Lawrence Furnace: A Historical Overview

The Development and Layout of Lawrence Furnace's Company Town

The establishment of Lawrence Furnace in the early 19th century necessitated the creation of a company town to house and support the workers essential to the furnace's operations. This town was deliberately situated close to the furnace to ensure that the workforce could easily commute to work, maximizing productivity and minimizing downtime. The town's layout was planned with the furnace at its core, surrounded by worker housing, a general store, a schoolhouse, and a church, reflecting the centrality of the furnace in the lives of the residents.

Housing in Lawrence Furnace's company town was practical and modest, consisting of small wooden cottages constructed by the furnace company. These homes provided essential shelter for the workers and their families, but they were basic in their amenities, reflecting the utilitarian needs of the workforce. Rent for these homes was often automatically deducted from workers' wages, creating a system where housing was inextricably linked to employment at the furnace.

The general store was a pivotal element of Lawrence Furnace's company town. Operated by the furnace company, the store was stocked with a variety of goods, including groceries, clothing, and other household necessities. Workers relied on the store for their everyday needs, and most transactions were conducted on credit, with the cost deducted from their paychecks. This system, while convenient, often led to a cycle of debt that was difficult for workers to escape, binding them economically to the company.

The town's schoolhouse provided basic education to the children of the workers. The curriculum focused on essential skills such as reading, writing, and arithmetic, preparing children for future employment, either at the furnace or in related industries. However, formal education was often limited, as older children were expected to contribute to the family income at a young age.

The church in Lawrence Furnace's company town played a vital role in the community. It was more than just a place of worship; it was a social and cultural center where residents gathered for religious services, social events, and mutual support. The church helped to foster a sense of community among the residents, providing spiritual guidance and emotional support in a challenging environment.

Life in Lawrence Furnace's Company Town

Life in the company town of Lawrence Furnace was closely tied to the demands of the furnace. Workers typically started their day early, with long shifts that were physically demanding and often hazardous. The intense heat, noise, and the ever-present danger of accidents made working at the furnace a challenging occupation. Despite these challenges, the work was a source of pride for many, as the iron produced at Lawrence Furnace contributed significantly to the industrial growth of the region.

After completing their shifts, workers returned to their homes within the company town. The general store was a key part of daily life, not just as a place to purchase goods but as a hub of social interaction where residents could exchange news and support each other. The reliance on the store for all necessities meant that workers had little financial flexibility, with much of their earnings going directly back to the furnace company.

Women in the company town played essential roles in maintaining the household, caring for children, and often contributing to the family income through domestic work or by taking in laundry. The division of labor was traditional, with men working in the furnace and women handling domestic responsibilities, but both roles were vital to the functioning of the household and the community.

Social life in the town revolved around the church and occasional community gatherings. The church organized events such as religious services, community meals, and holiday celebrations, which were important for maintaining morale and fostering a sense of belonging among the residents. These gatherings provided a respite from the hardships of daily life and helped to build a strong community spirit.

Challenges Faced by the Residents

Living and working in Lawrence Furnace's company town presented numerous challenges. The physical demands of working at the furnace were severe, with long hours, dangerous conditions, and little room for error. Injuries were common, and medical care was often inadequate, leading to long-term health problems for many workers. The harsh working environment took a toll not just on the workers' physical health but also on their mental well-being.

Economic challenges were also significant. The system of payment in company scrip, which could only be used at the company store, meant that workers were often trapped in a cycle of debt. This economic dependency on the furnace company made it difficult for workers to leave and seek better opportunities elsewhere, effectively tying their fortunes to the success of the furnace.

The limited availability of education and other social services meant that children often had to contribute to the family's income from a young age, limiting their opportunities for advancement. This perpetuated a cycle of poverty and dependence, as children followed in their parents' footsteps, working at the furnace and living in the company town.

Despite these hardships, the residents of Lawrence Furnace's company town demonstrated resilience and solidarity. The close-knit nature of the community provided a support network that was crucial for survival in such a demanding environment. Families and neighbors relied on each other for help with childcare, food, and emotional support, creating a strong sense of community in the face of adversity.

The Decline of Lawrence Furnace's Company Town

As the 19th century progressed, the iron industry in the Hanging Rock Iron Region began to decline, and Lawrence Furnace was no exception. The depletion of accessible iron ore deposits and the increasing difficulty of sourcing timber for charcoal production made it harder for the furnace to remain competitive. Additionally, advancements in iron production technology, particularly the rise of coke-fired blast furnaces, made the older charcoal furnaces like Lawrence less economically viable.

The closure of Lawrence Furnace had a profound impact on its company town. With the furnace no longer in operation, the town lost its primary source of employment and economic stability. Many residents were forced to leave in search of work elsewhere, leading to a gradual decline in the town's population. The general store, school, and church eventually closed, and the town's buildings fell into disrepair.

Today, little remains of Lawrence Furnace's company town. The buildings have long since disappeared, and the area has largely reverted to nature. However, the stories of the workers and their families who lived and worked in the town remain an important part of the region's history. These stories are a testament to the resilience and determination of the people who built their lives around the furnace, and they serve as a reminder of the challenges and hardships faced by those who contributed to the growth of the area.

The company town of Lawrence Furnace was more than just a place to live; it was a community built around the demands of the iron furnace. Life in the town was challenging, with residents facing physical, economic, and social hardships, yet they demonstrated remarkable resilience in the face of these difficulties. The decline of the iron industry brought an end to the town, but the legacy of its residents lives on in the history of the Hanging Rock Iron Region.

As we reflect on the history of Lawrence Furnace's company town, it is important to remember the contributions of the workers and their families. Their labor was essential to the growth of the iron industry and, by extension, to the industrialization of the United States. The stories of their lives offer valuable insights into the human side of industrial history and the communities that were shaped by the demands of the furnace.

Chapter 11

Iron Siblings: Madison and Monroe Furnaces' Shared Heritage

Madison and Monroe Furnaces and Their Shared Company Town: An Industrial Legacy

Madison and Monroe Furnaces: Twin Giants of the Hanging Rock Iron Region

Madison and Monroe Furnaces, located within the same forested area in Southern Ohio, are often referred to as "twin" furnaces due to their close proximity and interrelated operations. Both furnaces were significant contributors to the iron production in the Hanging Rock Iron Region during the 19th century, playing vital roles in the industrialization of the region. This document explores the history, operations, and legacy of these two furnaces, highlighting their importance in the broader context of the region's iron industry.

The Establishment of Madison Furnace

Madison Furnace was established in 1854 in Jackson County, Ohio, as part of the broader expansion of iron production in the Hanging Rock Iron Region. Named after President James Madison, the furnace was constructed using local materials, including limestone and sandstone, which were abundant in the area. The location was strategically chosen for its proximity to rich deposits of iron ore and vast forests that provided the wood necessary for producing charcoal, the primary fuel for the furnace.

Madison Furnace was designed as a cold-blast charcoal furnace, a common technology of the time, which involved blowing unheated air into the furnace to facilitate the smelting process. This method, though labor-intensive, produced high-quality pig iron that was in demand for various industrial applications, particularly in the railroad and construction industries.

The workforce at Madison Furnace consisted of skilled furnace operators, colliers (charcoal burners), miners, and laborers, many of whom lived in nearby company-owned housing. The furnace operated continuously, with workers maintaining the furnace around the clock to ensure a steady production of pig iron.

The Establishment of Monroe Furnace

Monroe Furnace, established in 1856, just two years after Madison Furnace, was located nearby within the same forested area of Jackson County. Like its "twin," Monroe Furnace was named after a U.S. president, James Monroe, and shared many of the same resources and operational characteristics as Madison Furnace.

Monroe Furnace was also a cold-blast charcoal furnace, relying on the same technology and resources as its neighbor. The two furnaces were closely linked, often sharing the same workforce and utilizing the same sources of iron ore and charcoal. The proximity of the two furnaces allowed for a collaborative approach to iron production, with both furnaces contributing to the overall output of the region.

The establishment of Monroe Furnace further solidified the importance of this area in the Hanging Rock Iron Region's iron industry, making it a significant center for iron production during the mid-19th century.

Operations and Interdependence

Madison and Monroe Furnaces operated in close cooperation, often sharing resources such as labor, raw materials, and transportation routes. The forests surrounding the furnaces provided the wood needed to produce charcoal, which was essential for smelting the iron ore. The iron ore itself was mined from nearby deposits and transported to the furnaces, where it was combined with charcoal and limestone in the furnace stacks.

The interdependence of the two furnaces was a key factor in their success. By working together, Madison and Monroe Furnaces were able to maintain a steady production of pig iron, which was then transported to markets via the Ohio River and various railroads. The collaboration between the two furnaces also allowed them to compete more effectively with other furnaces in the region, ensuring their continued operation during a time of intense competition and fluctuating market conditions.

The workforce at both furnaces was primarily composed of local laborers, many of whom had been working in the iron industry for generations. The close-knit communities that grew up around the furnaces were heavily reliant on the iron industry for their livelihoods, with entire families often working at the furnaces or in related industries such as mining and charcoal production.

Economic Impact and Decline

The economic impact of Madison and Monroe Furnaces on Jackson County and the broader Hanging Rock Iron Region was significant. The furnaces provided steady employment for hundreds of workers and supported the growth of local businesses that supplied goods and services to the furnaces and their employees. The iron produced at

Madison and Monroe Furnaces was used in a variety of applications, including the construction of railroads, machinery, and tools, all of which were essential to the industrial growth of the United States during the 19th century.

However, as the 19th century progressed, both Madison and Monroe Furnaces began to face significant challenges. The depletion of local timber resources made charcoal production increasingly difficult and expensive. Additionally, the rise of coke-fired blast furnaces, which were more efficient and produced higher-quality iron, made the older charcoal furnaces less competitive.

By the late 19th century, both Madison and Monroe Furnaces were struggling to remain profitable. Monroe Furnace ceased operations first, followed by Madison Furnace shortly thereafter. The closure of these furnaces marked the end of an era for the region and had a significant impact on the local communities that had depended on them for their livelihoods. Many workers were forced to leave the area in search of work elsewhere, leading to a decline in the local population and economy.

Legacy and Preservation

Today, the sites of Madison and Monroe Furnaces are recognized as important historical landmarks, though few physical remnants of the original structures remain. Efforts have been made to preserve what is left of the furnaces and to educate the public about their historical significance. Interpretive markers at the sites provide information about the history of the furnaces and their role in the development of the Hanging Rock Iron Region.

The legacy of Madison and Monroe Furnaces is preserved through ongoing research and documentation by local historians and preservationists. Artifacts and records related to the furnaces are displayed in local museums, where they serve as a testament to the region's rich industrial heritage. The stories of Madison and Monroe Furnaces are reminders of the hard work and ingenuity of the men and women who built and operated these furnaces, and of the vital role that the Hanging Rock Iron Region played in the industrialization of the United States.

In addition to their historical significance, the sites of Madison and Monroe Furnaces are part of a broader effort to preserve the industrial heritage of the Hanging Rock Iron Region. These furnaces are among several sites in the region that have been recognized for their importance in the history of American industry. Interpretive markers and educational programs help visitors understand the role that these furnaces played in the development of the United States and the impact they had on the lives of the people who lived and worked in the region.

Madison and Monroe Furnaces were twin pillars of the Hanging Rock Iron Region's iron industry during the 19th century. Their close proximity and interdependent operations allowed them to thrive in a highly competitive environment, contributing significantly to the economic development of Southern Ohio. Although both furnaces eventually succumbed to the challenges of the late 19th century, their legacy continues to be felt in the region today.

As we continue to explore the history of the Hanging Rock Iron Region, it is important to remember the contributions of furnaces like Madison and Monroe, whose stories are woven into the fabric of the region's industrial heritage. Their legacy serves as a reminder of the critical role that iron production played in the growth and development of the United States, and of the men and women who worked tirelessly to build a better future for themselves and their communities.

The operations of Madison and Monroe Furnaces were supported by a shared company town that grew around them. This town was not just a place of residence for workers but also an essential element of the furnaces' operations. Let's explore the life and community that made these furnaces possible.

The Company Town of Madison Furnace: A Historical Overview

The Founding and Early Development of Madison Furnace

Madison Furnace was established in 1854 during a period of rapid industrial expansion in the Hanging Rock Iron Region. The furnace was strategically located to take advantage of the abundant natural resources in the area, including timber for charcoal production and nearby iron ore deposits. The decision to establish a company town alongside the furnace was driven by the need to attract and retain a stable workforce in a relatively remote area.

The early development of Madison and Monroe Furnaces' company town was marked by careful planning and a focus on sustainability. Unlike some earlier company towns that were built quickly with little thought to long-term habitation, Madison and Monroe Furnaces' town was designed with an eye toward creating a lasting community. This included the construction of more permanent structures and the establishment of key institutions that would support the social and economic life of the town.

Unique Features of Madison and Monroe Furnaces' Company Town

One of the most distinctive features of Madison and Monroe Furnaces' company town was its integration with the surrounding natural landscape. The town was laid out in a way that took advantage of the natural topography, with homes and community buildings positioned to benefit from the natural shade and protection offered by the surrounding hills. This not only provided a measure of comfort for the residents but also helped to protect the town from the harsh elements.

The use of local materials in the construction of the town's buildings further tied the community to its environment. Homes were built using locally sourced timber and stone, giving the town a cohesive aesthetic that reflected its natural surroundings. The durability of these materials also meant that many of the town's structures were built to last, offering a higher standard of living than was found in some other company towns.

Another unique aspect of Madison and Monroe Furnaces' company town was its emphasis on self-sufficiency. The town included designated areas for gardens and small-scale farming, allowing residents to grow their own food and reduce their reliance on the company store. This focus on self-sufficiency was particularly important during periods of economic downturn, when wages might be reduced or when supplies were scarce.

Social and Cultural Life in Madison and Monroe Furnaces' Company Town

Social and cultural life in Madison and Monroe Furnaces' company town was shaped by a strong sense of community and a shared commitment to mutual support. The town's layout, with its central gathering spaces and close proximity of homes, fostered a sense of closeness among the residents. This was further reinforced by the presence of communal institutions such as the church and the meeting hall, which served as venues for social interaction, cultural events, and collective decision-making.

The church in Madison and Monroe Furnaces' company town played a central role not only as a place of worship but also as a hub for social activities. Religious services, community meetings, and celebrations were all held here, making it a focal point for the town's cultural life. The church also provided a space where residents could come together to address communal challenges, such as organizing mutual aid during difficult times or discussing issues related to the town's governance.

Education was another important aspect of life in Madison and Monroe Furnaces' company town. The town's schoolhouse was relatively well-equipped for its time, offering instruction not only to children but also to adults seeking to improve their literacy and skills. This emphasis on education reflected a broader recognition that a more informed and capable workforce could contribute to the long-term success of the furnace operations.

Challenges and Adaptations

Despite its strengths, life in Madison and Monroe Furnaces' company town was not without challenges. The physically demanding work at the furnace, coupled with the economic fluctuations that characterized the iron industry, meant that residents often faced periods of hardship. The remote location of the town also posed challenges, particularly when it came to accessing goods and services that were not available locally.

Economic challenges were a constant concern, especially during periods of reduced demand for iron or when the furnace was forced to cut back on production. These downturns often led to wage reductions and layoffs, making it difficult for families to make ends meet. However, the town's emphasis on self-sufficiency helped to mitigate some of these challenges, allowing residents to rely on their gardens and local resources to supplement their incomes.

Social cohesion was key to the town's ability to adapt to these challenges. The strong sense of community, reinforced by the town's institutions and social networks, provided residents with the support they needed to navigate difficult times. This included mutual aid arrangements, where neighbors would help each other with food, childcare, or other necessities, ensuring that no one was left to face hardship alone.

The Decline of Madison and Monroe Furnaces' Company Town

The decline of Madison Furnace began in the late 19th century, as the iron industry in the Hanging Rock Iron Region faced increasing competition from more modern production methods. By the 1880s, the furnace was struggling to remain profitable, and the economic pressures began to take a toll on the company town. As production slowed and wages were reduced, many residents were forced to leave in search of work elsewhere.

The town's emphasis on self-sufficiency provided some buffer against the decline, but ultimately, the economic realities were inescapable. As the furnace ceased operations, the town's population dwindled, and the once-thriving community began to disperse. Over time, the buildings fell into disrepair, and the town was gradually abandoned.

Today, little remains of Madison and Monroe Furnaces' company town. The structures have long since disappeared, and the area has largely returned to its natural state. However, the legacy of the town lives on in the stories of those who lived there and in the history of the Hanging Rock Iron Region. The town's unique approach to self-sufficiency, its integration with the natural landscape, and its strong sense of community set it apart from other company towns of the era.

Madison and Monroe Furnaces' company town was a testament to the resilience and ingenuity of its residents. Built with a focus on sustainability and self-sufficiency, the town offered a higher standard of living than many other company towns of the time. Its unique features, including the use of local materials, the integration with the natural landscape, and the emphasis on education and community support, made it a distinctive example of industrial-era planning.

As we reflect on the history of Madison and Monroe Furnaces' company town, it is important to recognize the contributions of its residents to the growth of the iron industry and to the development of community life in industrial America. Their experiences offer valuable insights into the interplay between industry, environment, and community, and they remind us of the human stories that are at the heart of our industrial heritage.

Chapter 12

Olive's Offering: The Narrative of Olive Furnace

Olive Furnace and Its Company Town: An Industrial Legacy

Olive Furnace: Comprehensive History

Olive Furnace, established in 1846 in Lawrence County, Ohio, was one of the many iron furnaces that contributed to the prominence of the Hanging Rock Iron Region during the 19th century. The furnace was named after Olive Massie, the daughter of Nathaniel Massie, a prominent surveyor and one of the early settlers in the region. The furnace played a significant role in the local economy, contributing to the industrialization of Southern Ohio and supporting the growth of nearby communities.

Founders and Early Development

Olive Furnace was founded by Thomas W. Means, a key figure in the iron industry who was involved in the development of several other furnaces in the region. The decision to establish Olive Furnace was driven by the availability of rich iron ore deposits in the surrounding hills, as well as the proximity to timber resources for charcoal production. The furnace was strategically located to take advantage of these resources, as well as to facilitate transportation via the Ohio River, which was essential for moving both goods and people.

The construction of Olive Furnace was a significant undertaking, requiring substantial investment and labor. The furnace was built as a charcoal-fired blast furnace, utilizing the cold-blast method that was common in the region at the time. The furnace's design included a large stone stack, which was used to house the smelting operations, and several outbuildings where charcoal was produced and stored.

Operations and Workforce

The operations at Olive Furnace were typical of the charcoal-fired furnaces in the Hanging Rock Iron Region. The furnace relied on a large workforce to mine the iron ore, produce the charcoal, and operate the furnace. At its peak, Olive Furnace employed around 150 workers, many of whom lived in company-owned housing near the furnace site.

The production process at Olive Furnace involved several stages. First, the iron ore was mined from the surrounding hills and transported to the furnace. The ore was then mixed with charcoal and limestone in the furnace stack, where it was heated to high temperatures to extract the iron. The molten iron was poured into molds to produce pig iron, which was then transported to markets via the Ohio River. The furnace operated continuously, with workers maintaining the furnace around the clock to ensure a steady and stable production of their goods.

The work at Olive Furnace was physically demanding and required long hours, especially for those involved in charcoal production and furnace operation. The process of producing charcoal was labor-intensive, involving the cutting down of trees, stacking the wood in large piles, and slowly burning it to create charcoal. The furnace also employed skilled workers, such as blacksmiths and carpenters, who were responsible for maintaining the furnace and its associated infrastructure.

Economic Impact

Olive Furnace played a crucial role in the economic development of Lawrence County. The furnace provided steady employment for hundreds of workers and supported the growth of local businesses that supplied goods and services to the furnace and its workers. The success of Olive Furnace also attracted additional investment into the region, leading to the establishment of other iron furnaces and related industries.

The iron produced at Olive Furnace was used in a variety of applications, including the construction of railroads, machinery, and tools, all of which were essential to the industrial growth of the United States during the 19th century. The furnace's operations also supported local agriculture, as farmers supplied food and other necessities to the growing population.

Decline and Closure

Like many other charcoal-fired furnaces in the region, Olive Furnace began to face challenges in the latter half of the 19th century. The depletion of local timber resources made charcoal production more difficult and expensive, while the rise of coke-fired furnaces, which were more efficient and produced higher-quality iron, made the older charcoal furnaces less competitive.

By the 1880s, Olive Furnace was struggling to remain profitable. The furnace eventually ceased operations in the late 1880s, marking the end of an era for Lawrence County. The closure of Olive Furnace had a significant impact on the local community, leading to job losses and economic decline. Many of the workers who had depended on the furnace for their livelihoods were forced to leave the area in search of work elsewhere.

Legacy and Preservation

Today, the site of Olive Furnace is recognized as a historical landmark, with remnants of the furnace still visible in the landscape. The site has been preserved with interpretive markers that provide information about the history of the furnace and its role in the development of the Hanging Rock Iron Region. Visitors to the site can explore the remains of the furnace and learn about the history of iron production in Southern Ohio.

The legacy of Olive Furnace is also preserved through ongoing research and documentation by local historians and preservationists. Artifacts and records related to the furnace are displayed in local museums, where they serve as a testament to the region's rich industrial heritage. The story of Olive Furnace is a reminder of the hard work and ingenuity of the men and women who built and operated the furnace, and of the vital role that the Hanging Rock Iron Region played in the industrialization of the United States.

Modern Legacy

In addition to its historical significance, the site of Olive Furnace is part of a broader effort to preserve the industrial heritage of the Hanging Rock Iron Region. The furnace is one of several sites in the region that have been recognized for their importance in the history of American industry. Interpretive markers and educational programs help visitors understand the role that these furnaces played in the development of the United States and the impact they had on the lives of the people who lived here and far away.

Olive Furnace's story is one of industrial success and decline, as well as community and resilience. The furnace helped shape the social and economic fabric of Lawrence County, leaving a lasting legacy that continues to be felt in the region today. As such, Olive Furnace remains an important part of Southern Ohio's cultural and historical identity.

The operations of Olive Furnace were supported by the company town that grew around it. This town was not just a place of residence for workers but also an essential element of the furnace's operations. Let's explore the life and community that made Olive Furnace possible.

The Company Town of Olive Furnace: A Historical Overview

The Structure of Olive Furnace's Company Town

The company town associated with Olive Furnace was designed to serve the needs of the workers and their families, ensuring a stable workforce for the furnace's operations. The town was located near the furnace to minimize travel time for the workers, and its layout included essential facilities such as worker housing, a general store, a schoolhouse, and a church. The town was constructed with the furnace as its focal point, reflecting its central role in the community.

Housing in Olive Furnace's company town was typical of the period, consisting of modest wooden homes built by the furnace company. These homes were functional, providing basic shelter for the workers and their families. The homes were rented to workers at a nominal fee, with rent often deducted directly from their wages. The close proximity of the housing to the furnace was a key feature, allowing workers to respond quickly to the demands of their jobs.

The general store in Olive Furnace's company town was a central part of daily life. Operated by the furnace company, the store stocked a wide range of essential goods, including food, clothing, and household items. Workers typically purchased these items on credit, with the costs deducted from their paychecks, creating an economic dependency on the company. The store was more than just a place to buy goods; it was a social hub where residents could gather, share news, and build a sense of community.

Education in the town was provided by a small schoolhouse. The school offered basic instruction in reading, writing, and arithmetic, primarily for the children of furnace workers. While education was valued, it was often cut short as older children were expected to contribute to the family income by working in the furnace or related industries.

The church in Olive Furnace's company town was a vital institution, supported by the furnace company. The church served as both a place of worship and a community gathering spot, offering religious services, social events, and mutual support. The church played a significant role in maintaining social cohesion and promoting moral behavior within the town, making it an essential part of community life.

Daily Life in the Company Town

Daily life in the company town of Olive Furnace was structured around the demanding schedule of the furnace. Workers typically began their day early in the morning, working long shifts that were physically exhausting and often dangerous. The work at the furnace exposed workers to extreme heat, hazardous materials, and the constant risk of injury, making it a challenging environment.

After their shifts, workers returned to their homes in the company town, where they spent time with their families and participated in community activities. The general store was a central part of daily life, not only as a place to buy goods but also as a social gathering spot.

The store was often the only source of goods for the residents, and its role in the community extended beyond commerce, serving as a place where people could connect and share news.

Women in the town played a crucial role in managing the household, caring for children, and often contributing to the family income through activities such as sewing, laundry, or working in the company store. The division of labor in the town was traditional, with men working at the furnace and women handling domestic tasks, but the women's contributions were essential to the functioning of the household and the community.

Social life in Olive Furnace's company town revolved around the church and community events. The church organized religious services, social gatherings, and celebrations, providing residents with opportunities to come together and strengthen their sense of community. The church's influence extended into all aspects of daily life, offering spiritual guidance and emotional support to the residents.

Social Life and Community

The residents of Olive Furnace's company town developed a strong sense of community, forged through their shared experiences of working at the furnace and living in close proximity. Social life in the town was centered around the church and the general store, both of which played crucial roles in the daily lives of the residents.

Community events, such as religious holidays, picnics, and dances, were highlights of social life in the town. These events provided much-needed relief from the demands of work and allowed residents to relax and enjoy each other's company. The church, as the town's social hub, was instrumental in organizing these events and fostering a sense of unity among the residents.

The general store, beyond being a place to purchase goods, was a focal point for social interaction. It was here that residents could catch up on the latest news, share stories, and discuss the challenges they faced in their daily lives. The store's role in the community was multifaceted, making it a key part of the town's social fabric.

Challenges and Hardships

Life in Olive Furnace's company town was not without its difficulties. The physically demanding work at the furnace, combined with the economic constraints of living in a company-owned town, placed significant stress on workers and their families. Health and safety were major concerns, as accidents and illnesses were common, and access to medical care was often limited.

The economic system of the company town, where workers were paid in company scrip that could only be used at the company store, further exacerbated the challenges faced by residents. This system created a cycle of debt and dependence, making it difficult for workers to leave the town or seek better opportunities elsewhere. The limited availability of education and other social services also meant that children were often expected to contribute to the family's income from a young age, perpetuating the cycle yet again.

Despite these challenges, the residents of the company town showed remarkable resilience. They developed close-knit communities where mutual support and solidarity were essential for survival. Families relied on each other for assistance, whether it was sharing food, helping with childcare, or providing moral support during difficult times. The church also played a vital role in offering spiritual and emotional support, helping residents cope with the challenges of daily life.

The Decline of Olive Furnace and Its Company Town

As the iron industry in the Hanging Rock Iron Region began to decline in the late 19th century, so too did the company town associated with Olive Furnace. The depletion of local resources, including timber for charcoal and accessible iron ore deposits, made it increasingly difficult for the furnace to remain profitable. Additionally, the rise of more efficient coke-fired blast furnaces in other regions reduced the competitiveness of charcoal furnaces like Olive.

The closure of Olive Furnace had a profound impact on the company town. Without the furnace to provide employment and economic stability, many residents were forced to leave in search of work elsewhere. The company store, school, and church gradually closed, and the town's population dwindled. Buildings fell into disrepair, and the once-thriving community became a ghost town, with only a few remnants of its former life remaining.

Today, the site of Olive Furnace's company town is largely forgotten, with few physical traces of its existence. However, the stories of the workers and their families who lived and worked in the town are an important part of the region's history. These stories serve as a reminder of the challenges and hardships faced by those who contributed to the development of the American iron industry, and of the resilience and determination that characterized life in the company towns of the Hanging Rock Iron Region.

The company town of Olive Furnace was a microcosm of the broader iron industry in the Hanging Rock Iron Region. It was a place where the demands of industrial production shaped every aspect of daily life, from work and housing to social and community activities. While life in the company town was often challenging and fraught with hardships, it was also marked by a strong sense of community and shared purpose.

As we look back on the history of the region, it is important to remember the contributions of the workers and their families who lived in these company towns. Their lives were inextricably linked to the furnaces that fueled the growth of the nation, and their stories are an essential part of the legacy of the Hanging Rock Iron Region. The decline of the company towns, like that of the iron industry itself, was a reflection of broader economic and technological changes, but the resilience and determination of the people and area.

Chapter 13

Union's Unity: The History of Union Furnace

Union Furnace and Its Company Town: An Industrial Legacy

Union Furnace: Comprehensive History

Union Furnace, established in 1826 in Lawrence County, Ohio, was one of the earliest iron furnaces in the Hanging Rock Iron Region. The furnace was developed by the Carpenter family, who played a significant role in the industrial growth of the region. Union Furnace was notable for its early adoption of new technologies and its contribution to the production of pig iron, which was essential to the United States' industrial expansion during the 19th century.

Founders and Early Development

Union Furnace was founded by the Carpenter family, who were prominent industrialists in the Hanging Rock Iron Region. The family recognized the potential of the area's rich iron ore deposits, abundant forests for charcoal production, and proximity to transportation routes like the Ohio River. The decision to establish Union Furnace was part of a broader strategy to capitalize on these resources and contribute to the burgeoning iron industry in Southern Ohio.

The construction of Union Furnace required significant investment and labor. The furnace was designed as a charcoal-fired blast furnace, utilizing the cold-blast method that was common in the region at the time. The furnace's stone stack, which housed the smelting operations, was constructed using locally sourced materials. The site was strategically chosen for its proximity to the necessary resources, ensuring efficient production and transportation of pig iron to markets across the country.

Operations and Workforce

Union Furnace was a major industrial operation that employed a substantial workforce to manage its complex processes. At its peak, the furnace employed around 150 workers, including miners, colliers (charcoal burners), furnace operators, and general laborers. These workers were typically housed in company-owned housing near the furnace site, forming a community that was heavily reliant on the furnace for economic stability.

The production process at Union Furnace involved several stages. First, the iron ore was mined from the surrounding hills and transported to the furnace. The ore was then combined with charcoal and limestone in the furnace stack, where it was heated to high temperatures to extract the iron. The cold-blast method, while labor-intensive, produced high-quality pig iron that was in great demand for various industrial applications.

The work at Union Furnace was physically demanding and required long hours, especially for those involved in charcoal production and furnace operation. The process of producing charcoal was particularly labor-intensive, as it involved the cutting down of trees, stacking the wood in large piles, and slowly burning it to create charcoal, which was then transported to the furnace. The furnace operated continuously, with workers maintaining the furnace around the clock to ensure a steady supply of pig iron.

Economic Impact

Union Furnace played a significant role in the economic development of Lawrence County and the broader Hanging Rock Iron Region. The furnace provided steady employment for hundreds of workers and supported the growth of local businesses that supplied goods and services to the furnace and its workers. The success of Union Furnace also attracted additional investment into the region, leading to the establishment of other iron furnaces and related industries.

The iron produced at Union Furnace was used in a variety of applications, including the construction of railroads, machinery, and tools, all of which were essential to the industrial growth of the United States during the 19th century. The furnace's operations also supported local agriculture, as farmers supplied food and other necessities to the growing population.

Technological Advancements and Adaptations

As with other furnaces in the region, Union Furnace adapted to technological advancements in the iron industry. Over time, the furnace incorporated new techniques and methods to improve efficiency and output. The introduction of the hot-blast method, which preheated the air before it was blown into the furnace, significantly improved the efficiency of the smelting process. This method allowed Union Furnace to produce larger quantities of higher-quality iron, making it more competitive in the rapidly expanding area.

The transition from charcoal to coke as the primary fuel for iron production was another significant advancement. Coke, made from coal, burned at higher temperatures than charcoal and was more abundant and less labor-intensive to produce. The adoption of coke-fired furnaces in the latter half of the 19th century helped Union Furnace maintain its position as a leading producer of pig iron, even as other furnaces in the region began to struggle with the challenges of resource depletion and competition.

Decline and Closure

Despite its success, Union Furnace eventually faced the same challenges that led to the decline of many other iron furnaces in the region. The depletion of local timber resources made charcoal production increasingly difficult and costly, even as the furnace began to rely more on coke. The rise of larger, more efficient steel mills in other parts of the country also put pressure on the Hanging Rock Iron Region's furnaces, which found it increasingly difficult to compete.

By the late 19th century, Union Furnace was struggling to maintain profitability. The furnace ceased operations by the early 1900s, marking the end of an era for Lawrence County. The closure of Union Furnace had a significant impact on the local community, leading to job losses and economic decline. Many workers who had depended on the furnace for their livelihoods were forced to move elsewhere in search of work, and the once-thriving community around the furnace began to dwindle.

Legacy and Preservation

Today, the site of Union Furnace is recognized as a historical landmark, though little remains of the original structure. Efforts have been made to preserve what is left of the furnace and to educate the public about its historical significance. Interpretive markers at the site provide information about the history of Union Furnace and its role in the development of the Hanging Rock Iron Region.

The legacy of Union Furnace is preserved through ongoing research and documentation by local historians and preservationists. Artifacts and records related to the furnace are displayed in local museums, where they serve as a testament to the region's rich industrial heritage. The story of Union Furnace is a reminder of the hard work and ingenuity of the men and women who built and operated the furnace, and of the vital role that the Hanging Rock Iron Region played in the industrialization of the United States.

Modern Legacy

In addition to its historical significance, the site of Union Furnace is part of a broader effort to preserve the industrial heritage of the Hanging Rock Iron Region. The furnace is one of several sites in the region that have been recognized for their importance in the history of American industry. Interpretive markers and educational programs help visitors understand the role that these furnaces played in the development of the United States and the impact they had on the lives of the people who lived there at the time.

Union Furnace's story is one of industrial success and decline, as well as community and resilience. The furnace helped shape the social and economic fabric of Lawrence County, leaving a lasting legacy that continues to be felt in the region today. As such, Union Furnace remains an important part of Southern Ohio's cultural and historical identity.

The operations of Union Furnace were supported by the company town that grew around it. This town was not just a place of residence for workers but also an essential element of the furnace's operations. Let's explore the life and community that made Union Furnace possible.

The Company Town of Union Furnace: A Historical Overview

The Structure of Union Furnace's Company Town

The company town associated with Union Furnace was developed to provide a self-sufficient environment for the workers and their families. Located close to the furnace itself, the town was carefully planned to include essential facilities such as housing, a general store, a schoolhouse, and a church. The layout of the town centered around the furnace, which was the primary employer and economic driver of the community.

Housing in the town was modest, reflecting the typical construction practices of the time. The wooden homes were small but functional, offering basic shelter for the workers and their families. The rent for these homes was deducted from the workers' wages, ensuring they remained close to their place of employment. The proximity of these homes to the furnace minimized travel time and allowed workers to quickly respond to the demands of the furnace.

The general store, operated by the furnace company, was the central hub of the town's economy. It provided residents with the necessary goods, including food, clothing, and household items. Purchases were often made on credit, with the cost deducted from workers' paychecks, creating an economic dependency on the furnace company. This system of credit often led to a cycle of debt that was difficult to escape, making it challenging for workers to save money or seek opportunities elsewhere.

Education in the town was provided by a small schoolhouse, where children received basic instruction in reading, writing, and arithmetic. The school was an important institution in the community, although education was often cut short as older children were expected to contribute to the family income by working in the furnace or related industries.

The church in Union Furnace's company town served as a central gathering place for the community. It was supported by the furnace company and played a significant role in maintaining social cohesion and promoting moral behavior among the residents. The church provided not only religious services but also a venue for social events and mutual support, making it a key part of community life.

Daily Life in the Company Town

Daily life in the company town of Union Furnace was dictated by the demanding schedule of the furnace. Workers typically began their day early in the morning, working long shifts that were physically exhausting and often dangerous. The work at the furnace exposed workers to extreme heat, hazardous materials, and the constant risk of injury, making it a challenging environment.

After their shifts, workers returned to their homes in the company town, where they spent time with their families and participated in community activities. The routine of daily life was shaped by the needs of the furnace, with the general store and church serving as central hubs for social interaction. Evenings were often spent attending church services, participating in social events, or simply relaxing at home with family.

Women in the town played a crucial role in managing the household, caring for children, and often contributing to the family income through activities such as sewing, laundry, or working in the company store. The division of labor was traditional, with men working at the furnace and women handling domestic responsibilities, but both roles were vital to the functioning of the household and the community.

The general store was an integral part of daily life, as it was the primary source of goods for the residents. The practice of buying on credit meant that many families lived with little financial security, and the economic dependence on the furnace company reinforced the power dynamics within the town.

Social Life and Community

Despite the challenges of life in the company town, the residents of Union Furnace developed a strong sense of community. The shared experience of working at the furnace, combined with the close-knit nature of the town, fostered a bond among residents. Social life in the town centered around the church and community events, which provided opportunities for residents to come together, share news, and support each other.

Community celebrations, such as religious holidays, picnics, and dances, were highlights of social life in the town. These events offered a welcome break from the demands of work and allowed residents to relax and enjoy each other's company. The church, as the social hub of the town, played a key role in organizing these events and fostering a sense of unity among the residents.

Education, while limited, was also an important aspect of community life. The schoolhouse in the town provided basic education to the children of workers, with the goal of preparing them for eventual work in the furnace or related industries. Although education was often cut short by the need for children to contribute to the family income, the school was a valued institution within the community.

Challenges and Hardships

Life in Union Furnace's company town was not without its difficulties. The physically demanding nature of the work at the furnace, combined with the economic constraints of living in a company-owned town, placed significant stress on workers and their families. Health and safety were major concerns, as accidents and illnesses were common, and access to medical care was often limited.

The economic system of the company town, where workers were paid in company scrip that could only be used at the company store, further exacerbated the challenges faced by residents. This system created a cycle of debt and dependence, making it difficult for workers to leave the town or seek better opportunities elsewhere. The limited availability of education and other social services also meant that children were often expected to contribute to the family's income from a young age, perpetuating the cycle.

Despite these challenges, the residents of the company town showed remarkable resilience. They developed close-knit communities where mutual support and solidarity were essential for survival. Families relied on each other for assistance, whether it was sharing food, helping with childcare, or providing moral support during difficult times. The church also played a vital role in offering spiritual and emotional support, helping residents cope with the challenges of daily life.

The Decline of Union Furnace and Its Company Town

As the iron industry in the Hanging Rock Iron Region began to decline in the late 19th century, so too did the company town associated with Union Furnace. The depletion of local resources, including timber for charcoal and accessible iron ore deposits, made it increasingly difficult for the furnace to remain profitable. Additionally, the rise of more efficient coke-fired blast furnaces in other regions reduced the competitiveness of charcoal furnaces like Union.

The closure of Union Furnace had a profound impact on the company town. Without the furnace to provide employment and economic stability, many residents were forced to leave in search of work elsewhere. The company store, school, and church gradually closed, and the town's population dwindled. Buildings fell into disrepair, and the once-thriving community became a ghost town, with only a few remnants of its former life remaining.

Today, the site of Union Furnace's company town is largely forgotten, with few physical traces of its existence. However, the stories of the workers and their families who lived and worked in the town are an important part of the region's history. These stories serve as a reminder of the challenges and hardships faced by those who contributed to the development of the American iron industry, and of the resilience and determination that characterized life in the company towns of the Hanging Rock Iron Region.

The company town of Union Furnace was a microcosm of the broader iron industry in the Hanging Rock Iron Region. It was a place where the demands of industrial production shaped every aspect of daily life, from work and housing to social and community activities. While life in the company town was often challenging and fraught with hardships, it was also marked by a strong sense of community and shared purpose.

As we look back on the history of the region, it is important to remember the contributions of the workers and their families who lived in these company towns. Their lives were inextricably linked to the furnaces that fueled the growth of the nation, and their stories are an essential part of the legacy of the Hanging Rock Iron Region. The decline of the company towns, like that of the iron industry itself, was a reflection of broader economic and technological changes, but the resilience and determination of workers will always remain.

Chapter 14

Vesuvius Rises: The Story of Vesuvius Furnace

Vesuvius Furnace and Its Company Town: An Industrial Legacy

Vesuvius Furnace: Comprehensive History

Vesuvius Furnace, established in 1833 in Lawrence County, Ohio, was one of the most significant and well-known iron furnaces in the Hanging Rock Iron Region. Named after the famous Mount Vesuvius in Italy, the furnace was known for its size, output, and role in the region's industrial growth. Founded by the Carpenter family, Vesuvius Furnace became a cornerstone of Southern Ohio's iron industry during the 19th century, contributing to the economic development of the region and the broader United States.

Founders and Early Development

The Carpenter family, who were among the prominent industrialists in the Hanging Rock Iron Region, founded Vesuvius Furnace in 1833. The family recognized the potential of the region's abundant natural resources—rich deposits of iron ore, vast forests for charcoal production, and proximity to the Ohio River, which facilitated transportation. Vesuvius Furnace was constructed using local stone, with a large chimney stack to vent the gases produced during smelting, a common design for blast furnaces of the area.

Vesuvius Furnace was strategically located near the resources necessary for iron production. The furnace was initially designed as a charcoal-fired blast furnace, utilizing the cold-blast method where unheated air was blown into the furnace to aid the smelting process. This method, while labor-intensive, was effective in producing high-quality pig iron, which was in great demand for various industrial applications, including railroads, machinery, and construction materials.

Operations and Workforce

Vesuvius Furnace was a large-scale operation, employing a significant workforce to manage its complex processes. At its peak, the furnace employed over 200 workers, including skilled furnace operators, colliers (charcoal burners), miners, and general laborers. The workers were typically housed in nearby company-owned housing, forming a community that revolved around the furnace's operations.

The production process at Vesuvius Furnace involved several stages, beginning with the mining of iron ore from nearby hills. The ore was transported to the furnace, where it was combined with charcoal and limestone in the furnace stack. The cold-blast method was initially used, but as technology advanced, the furnace adopted the hot-blast method, which involved preheating the air before it was introduced into the furnace. This technological advancement significantly improved the efficiency of the smelting.

The work at Vesuvius Furnace was physically demanding and required long hours, especially for those involved in charcoal production and furnace operation. The furnace operated continuously, with shifts of workers maintaining the furnace around the clock to ensure a steady supply of pig iron. The charcoal production process was particularly labor-intensive, as it involved cutting down trees, stacking the wood in large piles, and slowly burning it to create charcoal, which was then transported to the furnaace.

Vesuvius Furnace was known for the quality of its pig iron, which was highly valued in the market. The iron produced at the furnace was used in various industries, including the production of railroad ties, tools, and machinery, all of which were essential to the United States' industrial expansion during the 19th century.

Economic Impact

Vesuvius Furnace had a profound impact on the local economy, providing employment and supporting the growth of infrastructure in Lawrence County. The success of the furnace attracted additional investment into the region, leading to the establishment of other iron furnaces and related industries. The furnace's operations were closely tied to the development of transportation networks, including roads and canals, which facilitated the movement of raw materials and finished products.

The furnace also played a significant role in the broader economic development of the Hanging Rock Iron Region. The iron produced at Vesuvius Furnace was transported via the Ohio River to markets across the United States, contributing to the region's reputation as a leading producer of iron. The furnace's success also supported local businesses and services, from blacksmiths and carpenters to general stores and schools, all of which depended on the furnace's operations for their livelihood.

Technological Advancements and Adaptations

Over time, Vesuvius Furnace adapted to technological advancements in the iron industry. The introduction of the hot-blast method, which preheated the air before it was blown into the furnace, significantly improved the efficiency of the smelting process. This method allowed Vesuvius Furnace to produce larger quantities of higher-quality iron, making it more competitive in the rapidly evolving industry.

The transition from charcoal to coke as the primary fuel for iron production was another significant advancement. Coke, made from coal, burned at higher temperatures than charcoal and was more abundant and less labor-intensive to produce. The adoption of coke-fired furnaces in the latter half of the 19th century helped Vesuvius Furnace maintain its position as a leading producer of pig iron, even as other furnaces in the region began to struggle with the challenges of resource depletion and competition.

Decline and Closure

Despite its success, Vesuvius Furnace eventually faced the same challenges that led to the decline of many other iron furnaces in the region. The depletion of local timber resources made charcoal production increasingly difficult and costly, even as the furnace began to rely more on coke. The rise of larger, more efficient steel mills in other parts of the country also put pressure on the Hanging Rock Iron Region's furnaces, which found it increasingly difficult to compete.

By the 1890s, Vesuvius Furnace was struggling to maintain profitability. The furnace ceased operations at the end of the decade, marking the end of an era for Lawrence County. The closure of Vesuvius Furnace had a significant impact on the local community, leading to job losses and economic decline. Many workers who had depended on the furnace for their livelihoods were forced to move elsewhere in search of work, and the once-thriving community around the furnace began to dwindle.

Legacy and Preservation

Today, Vesuvius Furnace is remembered as one of the most important iron furnaces in the Hanging Rock Iron Region. The site of the furnace, now part of the Vesuvius Furnace Historical Area within the Wayne National Forest, is preserved as a historical landmark. Visitors can explore the remnants of the furnace, including the stone stack and other structures, along with interpretive trails that provide insights into the history of iron production in the region.

The legacy of Vesuvius Furnace is also preserved through ongoing research and documentation by local historians and preservationists. Artifacts and records related to the furnace are displayed in local museums, where they serve as a testament to the region's rich industrial heritage. The story of Vesuvius Furnace is a reminder of the hard work and ingenuity of the men and women who built and operated the furnace, and of the vital role that the Hanging Rock Iron Region played in the industrialization of this area and others near and far.

Modern Legacy

The site of Vesuvius Furnace continues to be a focal point for those interested in the history of the iron industry in Southern Ohio. Educational programs and guided tours help visitors understand the importance of the furnace and its impact on the local community. The preservation of the furnace and its surrounding area is part of a broader effort to celebrate and protect the industrial heritage of the Hanging Rock Iron Region.

Vesuvius Furnace's story is one of innovation, adaptation, and resilience. The furnace not only contributed to the economic development of Lawrence County but also played a crucial role in the broader narrative of America's industrial growth. As such, Vesuvius Furnace remains an enduring symbol of the ingenuity and determination that characterized the early industrial pioneers of Southern Ohio.

The operations of Vesuvius Furnace were supported by the company town that grew around it. This town was not just a place of residence for workers but also an essential element of the furnace's operations. Let's explore the life and community that made Vesuvius Furnace possible.

The Company Town of Vesuvius Furnace: A Historical Overview

The Strategic Significance and Establishment of Vesuvius Furnace

Vesuvius Furnace, established in 1833, was one of the earliest and most significant iron furnaces in the Hanging Rock Iron Region. Its strategic location near rich deposits of iron ore and abundant timber for charcoal production made it a key player in the early industrialization of southern Ohio. The furnace's success necessitated the creation of a company town to house the large workforce required to keep the furnace running efficiently.

The town that developed around Vesuvius Furnace was designed with the needs of both the workers and the furnace in mind. Unlike some of the smaller furnaces in the region, Vesuvius required a larger, more organized community to support its operations. The town was laid out with a clear hierarchy, reflecting the social and economic status of its residents, from the workers who toiled in the furnace to the managers who oversaw its operations.

Unique Characteristics of Vesuvius Furnace's Company Town

One of the most notable features of Vesuvius Furnace's company town was its scale. As one of the largest furnaces in the region, Vesuvius required a substantial workforce, and the town that grew up around it reflected this need. The town included not only worker housing but also a range of amenities that were uncommon in smaller company towns. These included a well-equipped general store, a dedicated schoolhouse, and even a small medical clinic to care for injured or ill workers.

The housing in Vesuvius Furnace's company town was also more varied than in other towns. While most workers lived in simple, functional homes, the town also featured larger, more comfortable houses for the furnace's managers and key personnel. These homes were often located on higher ground, away from the noise and smoke of the furnace, reflecting the social stratification within the town.

Another distinctive aspect of the town was its focus on education and training. Recognizing the importance of a skilled workforce, the furnace company invested in the education of both children and adults. The schoolhouse in Vesuvius Furnace's company town was one of the better-equipped in the region, offering a more comprehensive curriculum than was typical for the time. In addition to basic literacy and arithmetic, the school also provided instruction in technical skills that were directly applicable to the residents.

Social Life and Community Dynamics

The social life of Vesuvius Furnace's company town was shaped by the diverse backgrounds of its residents. The town attracted workers from various parts of the United States and even from Europe, leading to a rich tapestry of cultural influences. This diversity was reflected in the town's social activities, which included a wide range of cultural and religious events.

The church in Vesuvius Furnace's company town was a central institution, not only for worship but also as a gathering place for social events. The church hosted regular services as well as weddings, funerals, and community meetings, making it a focal point for the town's social life. The town's diversity was also evident in the variety of religious denominations represented, with the church often serving as a shared space for different congregations.

Recreation played an important role in the lives of the town's residents, providing a necessary counterbalance to the hard work at the furnace. Sports, music, and communal gatherings were common, and the town's residents took pride in organizing events that brought the community together. The larger size of the town meant that it could support more organized recreational activities, including a town band and occasional theatrical performances.

The hierarchical nature of the town also influenced its social dynamics. While there was a clear distinction between workers and management, there was also a strong sense of mutual dependency. The success of the furnace depended on the hard work and cooperation of all residents, creating a sense of shared purpose that helped to bridge social divides.

Challenges and Economic Pressures

Despite its advantages, life in Vesuvius Furnace's company town was not without challenges. The furnace's success was closely tied to the fluctuations of the iron market, and economic downturns often led to periods of hardship for the town's residents. Wages could be reduced, and layoffs were not uncommon during periods of low demand for iron.

The demanding nature of the work at the furnace also took a toll on the workers. The heat, noise, and physical strain of the job were constant, and accidents were a regular occurrence. While the presence of a medical clinic provided some relief, it was often insufficient to address the full range of injuries and health issues that arose from the work.

Social tensions could also arise, particularly between different ethnic and cultural groups within the town. While the town's diversity was generally a source of strength, it could also lead to misunderstandings and conflicts, especially during times of economic stress. However, the strong sense of community and shared purpose usually prevailed, helping to maintain social cohesion even during difficult times.

The Decline and Legacy of Vesuvius Furnace's Company Town

The decline of Vesuvius Furnace began in the late 19th century, as newer, more efficient iron production methods made older furnaces like Vesuvius increasingly obsolete. The economic pressures of the time, coupled with the depletion of local resources, led to the eventual closure of the furnace. As the furnace ceased operations, the company town began to decline as well, with many residents leaving in search of work elsewhere.

By the early 20th century, Vesuvius Furnace's company town was largely abandoned. The buildings fell into disrepair, and the once-thriving community was reduced to a shadow of its former self. However, the legacy of Vesuvius Furnace and its company town lives on in the history of the region. The site of the furnace has been preserved as part of a state park, offering visitors a glimpse into the past and a chance to learn about the important role that the furnace and its town played in the industrial development.

The stories of those who lived and worked in Vesuvius Furnace's company town continue to be an important part of the cultural heritage of the Hanging Rock Iron Region. The town's emphasis on education, community, and social cohesion set it apart from other company towns of the era, making it a unique example of industrial-era living.

Vesuvius Furnace's company town was a significant part of the iron industry in the Hanging Rock Iron Region. Its size, diversity, and emphasis on education and community made it a distinctive example of a company town, offering insights into the social and economic dynamics of the time. While the town ultimately declined along with the furnace, its legacy continues to be felt in the history of the region.

As we reflect on the history of Vesuvius Furnace's company town, it is important to recognize the contributions of its residents to the growth of the iron industry and to the development of community life in industrial America. Their experiences offer valuable lessons about the challenges and opportunities of industrialization, and they remind us of the human stories that are at the heart of our industrial heritage.

Chapter 15

Washington's Will: The Tale of Washington Furnace

Washington Furnace and Its Company Town: An Industrial Legacy

Washington Furnace: Comprehensive History

Washington Furnace, established in 1853 in Scioto County, Ohio, was one of the later iron furnaces built in the Hanging Rock Iron Region. Named in honor of the first U.S. President, George Washington, the furnace played a significant role in the region's iron production during the mid-19th century. Washington Furnace contributed to the industrial growth of the United States during a period of rapid economic expansion, particularly in the construction of railroads and the manufacturing of tools and machinery.

Founders and Early Development

Washington Furnace was founded by a group of investors and industrialists who recognized the potential of the region's rich iron ore deposits, abundant forests for charcoal production, and access to transportation routes like the Ohio River. The furnace was constructed using local stone and was designed as a charcoal-fired blast furnace, utilizing the cold-blast method that was common in the region at the time.

The site for Washington Furnace was strategically chosen to optimize access to the necessary resources. The surrounding hills provided rich deposits of iron ore, while the dense forests supplied the wood needed to produce charcoal. The furnace's location near transportation routes facilitated the movement of pig iron to markets throughout the United States.

Operations and Workforce

Washington Furnace was a significant industrial operation that employed a substantial workforce to manage its various processes. At its peak, the furnace employed around 150 workers, including skilled furnace operators, colliers (charcoal burners), miners, and general laborers. The workers were typically housed in company-owned housing near the furnace site, forming a community that was heavily reliant on the furnace for economic stability.

The production process at Washington Furnace involved several stages. First, iron ore was mined from the surrounding hills and transported to the furnace. The ore was then combined with charcoal and limestone in the furnace stack, where it was heated to high temperatures to extract the iron. The cold-blast method was initially used, where unheated air was blown into the furnace to aid the smelting process. This method, while labor-intensive, produced high-quality pig iron that was in great demand for various local industries.

The work at Washington Furnace was physically demanding and required long hours, especially for those involved in charcoal production and furnace operation. The process of producing charcoal was particularly labor-intensive, involving the cutting down of trees, stacking the wood in large piles, and slowly burning it to create charcoal, which was then transported to the furnace. The furnace operated continuously, with shifts of workers maintaining the furnace around the clock to ensure a steady supply of needed goods.

Economic Impact

Washington Furnace played a significant role in the economic development of Scioto County and the broader Hanging Rock Iron Region. The furnace provided steady employment for hundreds of workers and supported the growth of local businesses that supplied goods and services to the furnace and its workers. The success of

Washington Furnace also attracted additional investment into the region, leading to the establishment of other iron furnaces and related industries.

The iron produced at Washington Furnace was used in a variety of applications, including the construction of railroads, machinery, and tools, all of which were essential to the industrial growth of the United States during the 19th century. The furnace's operations also supported local agriculture, as farmers supplied food and other necessities to the growing population.

Decline and Closure

As the 19th century progressed, Washington Furnace, like many other charcoal-fired furnaces in the region, began to face significant challenges. The depletion of local timber resources made charcoal production increasingly difficult and expensive. Additionally, the rise of coke-fired blast furnaces, which were more efficient and produced higher-quality iron, made the older charcoal furnaces less competitive.

By the late 19th century, Washington Furnace was struggling to remain profitable. The furnace eventually ceased operations in the 1880s, marking the end of an era for Scioto County. The closure of Washington Furnace had a significant impact on the local community, leading to job losses and economic decline. Many of the workers who had depended on the furnace for their livelihoods were forced to leave the area in search of work elsewhere.

Legacy and Preservation

Today, the site of Washington Furnace is recognized as a historical landmark, though few remnants of the original structure remain. Efforts have been made to preserve what is left of the furnace and to educate the public about its historical significance. Interpretive markers at the site provide information about the history of Washington Furnace and its role in the development of the Hanging Rock Iron Region.

The legacy of Washington Furnace is preserved through ongoing research and documentation by local historians and preservationists. Artifacts and records related to the furnace are displayed in local museums, where they serve as a testament to the region's rich industrial heritage. The story of Washington Furnace is a reminder of the hard work and ingenuity of the men and women who built and operated the furnace, and of the vital role that the Hanging Rock Iron Region played in the industrialization of the expanding United States.

Modern Legacy

In addition to its historical significance, the site of Washington Furnace is part of a broader effort to preserve the industrial heritage of the Hanging Rock Iron Region. The furnace is one of several sites in the region that have been recognized for their importance in the history of American industry. Interpretive markers and educational programs help visitors understand the role that these furnaces played in the development of the United States and the impact they had on the lives of the people who developed this area.

Washington Furnace's story is one of industrial success and decline, as well as community and resilience. The furnace helped shape the social and economic fabric of Scioto County, leaving a lasting legacy that continues to be felt in the region today. As such, Washington Furnace remains an important part of Southern Ohio's cultural and historical identity.

The operations of Washington Furnace were supported by the company town that grew around it. This town was not just a place of residence for workers but also an essential element of the furnace's operations. Let's explore the life and community that made Washington Furnace possible.

The Company Town of Washington Furnace: A Historical Overview

The Establishment and Unique Features of Washington Furnace's Company Town

Founded in 1853, Washington Furnace quickly became a significant contributor to the iron industry in the Hanging Rock Iron Region. To accommodate the workers needed to operate the furnace, a company town was meticulously planned and constructed nearby. This town was more than just a collection of buildings; it was a community designed to sustain the workforce and their families in an era when transportation options were limited.

The residences in Washington Furnace's company town were built with practicality in mind. While the structures were indeed simple, they reflected the architectural trends of the mid-19th century, with sturdy frames and functional layouts that provided much-needed shelter for the workers' families. These homes, though modest, were often tailored to the needs of larger families, ensuring that multiple generations could live under one roof. The proximity of these homes to the furnace meant that workers could easily arrive for their long, hard, slave-like shifts.

At the heart of the town was the general store, a vital institution that went beyond mere commerce. Managed by the furnace company, this store was stocked with a diverse range of goods, from foodstuffs to work clothing, ensuring that the residents had access to everything they needed without having to venture far from the town. The store operated on a credit system, with purchases being deducted from the workers' wages. This practice, while convenient, often resulted in a cycle of debt that kept families without hope.

The schoolhouse, another cornerstone of the town, served as both an educational facility and a community center. Children of the workers received instruction in basic literacy and arithmetic, with the goal of preparing them for the workforce. However, the school also functioned as a meeting place for town events, further solidifying its role as a central part of life in Washington Furnace's company town.

The church in Washington Furnace's company town was more than just a place of worship; it was the spiritual and social heart of the community. Supported by the furnace company, the church provided a space for religious services, social gatherings, and community support. It was here that residents came together not only to practice their faith but also to celebrate milestones and support one another through the hardships of life in a company town.

Everyday Life in Washington Furnace's Company Town

Daily life in Washington Furnace's company town was a blend of hard work and community spirit. The demands of the furnace dictated the rhythm of life, with workers often beginning their day before dawn to manage the intensive labor required by iron production. The work was grueling, with long hours spent in extreme heat and constant exposure to potential hazards. Despite the challenges, the workers of Washington Furnace took pride in their contributions to the burgeoning iron industry that was vital to the development of this region and our nation.

After the workday, the company town provided a refuge where workers could relax and spend time with their families. The general store was not only a place to purchase necessities but also a social hub where residents could catch up on local news and enjoy a sense of camaraderie. The credit system at the store, while a source of economic pressure, also fostered a sense of mutual dependency that strengthened community bonds.

Women in the town played critical roles in maintaining households and contributing to the family income through a variety of means, including taking in boarders, sewing, and other domestic work. Their contributions were essential to the survival and well-being of their families, particularly in a setting where every member of the household was expected to contribute.

Social life in the company town centered around the church and the schoolhouse, which hosted a variety of events ranging from religious services to community celebrations. These gatherings were essential in providing a break from the daily grind and in maintaining the strong social fabric of the town. The church, in particular, was a source of comfort and support, offering spiritual guidance and a sense of community that was crucial for enduring the rigors of life in an industrial town.

Challenges and Adaptations

Living in Washington Furnace's company town was not without its challenges. The physically demanding work at the furnace was only one aspect of the difficulties faced by the residents. The economic system, where wages were often paid in company scrip usable only at the company store, created a dependency that many found difficult to escape. This system kept families tied to the company, as leaving the town meant leaving behind both employment and the economic credit system they relied on.

Health and safety were constant concerns, with accidents and illnesses being common due to the hazardous nature of the work and the lack of advanced medical care. The town's isolation also meant that residents had limited access to outside resources, relying heavily on what was provided by the furnace company.

Despite these obstacles, the residents of Washington Furnace's company town demonstrated remarkable resilience. They adapted to the challenges by creating a close-knit community where mutual aid and support were essential. The shared experiences of work, worship, and daily life fostered a strong sense of solidarity among the residents, helping them to endure the hardships and find meaning in their lives.

The Decline of Washington Furnace's Company Town

The decline of Washington Furnace began in the latter part of the 19th century, as the iron industry in the Hanging Rock Iron Region faced increasing competition and technological changes. The furnace, like many others in the region, struggled to compete with newer, more efficient methods of iron production, particularly those using coke rather than charcoal. By the 1880s, the economic pressures had become insurmountable, leading to the eventual closure of the furnace.

With the furnace no longer in operation, the company town lost its primary reason for existence. The population dwindled as workers and their families moved away in search of new opportunities. The once-bustling general store closed its doors, and the schoolhouse and church, which had been the heart of the community, were abandoned. Over time, the town's buildings fell into disrepair, and nature began to reclaim the land.

Today, little remains of Washington Furnace's company town. The physical structures may have disappeared, but the stories of those who lived and worked there are a vital part of the history of the Hanging Rock Iron Region. These stories remind us of the resilience and determination of the people who built their lives around the furnace and of the community that they created in the face of adversity.

Washington Furnace's company town was more than just a place to live and work; it was a community built around the demands of the iron industry. The residents faced numerous challenges, from the harsh working conditions to the economic pressures of the company store system, yet they forged a strong community that provided support and solidarity. The decline of the furnace brought an end to the town, but the legacy of its residents lives on in the history of the region.

As we reflect on the history of Washington Furnace's company town, it is important to remember the contributions of the workers and their families. Their labor was essential to the growth of the iron industry and the industrialization of the United States. The stories of their lives offer valuable insights into the human side of industrial history and the communities that were shaped by the demands of the furnace.

Chapter 16

Center Stage: The History of Center Furnace

Center Furnace: From The Perimeter

Center Furnace: Comprehensive History

Center Furnace, established in 1837 in Lawrence County, Ohio, was one of the early iron furnaces in the Hanging Rock Iron Region, an area that became a significant center of iron production in the 19th century. The furnace was founded by Theodore F. Rogers and John Campbell, two influential figures in the region's industrial development. Located in an area rich with natural resources, including iron ore, limestone, and timber, Center Furnace played a crucial role in the early industrialization of Southern Ohio and bordering regions of Kentucky and West Virginia.

Founders and Early Development

Theodore F. Rogers and John Campbell were among the pioneers of the iron industry in Southern Ohio. Their decision to establish Center Furnace was driven by the region's abundant natural resources and the growing demand for iron products in the United States. The furnace was strategically located near essential resources: iron ore deposits were plentiful in the surrounding hills, and the dense forests provided ample wood for charcoal production, which was the primary fuel for the furnace.

Center Furnace was designed as a charcoal-fired blast furnace, a common design in the mid-19th century. The furnace's construction was a significant undertaking, requiring substantial investment and labor. The blast furnace was built to be durable and efficient, with a large stone structure that housed the smelting operations. The furnace's location near the Ohio River also facilitated the transportation of pig iron to markets across the country.

Operations and Workforce

The operations at Center Furnace were typical of the charcoal-fired furnaces of the time. The furnace used a cold-blast method, where unheated air was blown into the furnace to aid in the smelting process. The iron ore, mixed with charcoal and limestone, was heated to high temperatures, causing the iron to separate from the ore and flow into molds to form pig iron. This pig iron was then transported to foundries and manufacturing plants, where it was further processed into various iron products.

The workforce at Center Furnace was diverse, including skilled furnace operators, colliers (charcoal burners), miners, and general laborers. At its peak, the furnace employed over 150 workers. The work was physically demanding and required long hours, especially for those involved in charcoal production and furnace operation. The workers were typically housed in nearby company-owned housing, forming a community centered around the furnace.

The furnace operated continuously, with shifts of workers maintaining the furnace around the clock. The charcoal production process was particularly labor-intensive, as it involved cutting down trees, stacking the wood in large piles, and slowly burning it to create charcoal, which was then transported to the furnace. The entire operation was carefully coordinated to ensure a steady supply of charcoal and iron ore, which was critical to keeping the furnace running efficiently.

Economic Impact

Center Furnace had a significant impact on the local economy, providing employment and supporting the development of infrastructure in the region. The furnace's success attracted additional investment into Lawrence County, leading to the establishment of other iron furnaces and related industries. The iron produced at Center Furnace was used in a variety of applications, including the construction of railroads, machinery, and tools, all of which were essential to the industrial growth of the United States.

The success of Center Furnace also led to improvements in transportation infrastructure. Roads were built and maintained to facilitate the movement of raw materials and finished products, and the nearby Ohio River served as a vital transportation route for shipping pig iron to markets in Cincinnati, Pittsburgh, and beyond.

Decline and Closure

By the late 19th century, Center Furnace, like many other charcoal-fired furnaces in the region, began to face significant challenges. The depletion of local timber resources made charcoal production increasingly difficult and expensive. Additionally, the rise of coke-fired blast furnaces, which were more efficient and produced higher-quality iron, made the older charcoal furnaces less competitive.

The economic pressures on Center Furnace continued to mount, and by the late 1870s, the furnace was no longer able to operate profitably. The furnace ceased operations, marking the end of an era for Lawrence County. The closure of Center Furnace had a profound impact on the local community, leading to job losses and economic decline. Many of the workers who had depended on the furnace for their livelihoods were forced to leave the area in search of work elsewhere.

Legacy and Preservation

Today, the site of Center Furnace is part of the Wayne National Forest, where remnants of the furnace can still be seen. The site is preserved as a historical landmark, with interpretive markers that provide visitors with information about the furnace's history and its role in the development of the Hanging Rock Iron Region.

The legacy of Center Furnace is remembered as a key part of Southern Ohio's industrial heritage. The furnace's contribution to the early industrialization of the United States, as well as its impact on the local community, continues to be studied and celebrated by historians and preservationists. The site remains a testament to the hard work and ingenuity of the men and women who built and operated the furnace, and it serves as a reminder of the region's rich industrial past.

Modern Legacy

The modern legacy of Center Furnace is also reflected in the continued interest in the region's industrial history. Local museums and historical societies have preserved artifacts and records related to the furnace, ensuring that future generations can learn about the importance of the iron industry in shaping Southern Ohio. The site of Center Furnace, along with other furnaces in the region, is part of a broader effort to preserve and promote the industrial heritage of the Hanging Rock Iron Region.

Chapter 17

Etna's Epoch: The Legacy of Etna Furnace

Etna Furnace: The Beginnings of Fire

Etna Furnace: Comprehensive History

Etna Furnace, established in 1832 in Lawrence County, Ohio, was one of the earliest and most significant iron furnaces in the Hanging Rock Iron Region. Founded by Thomas James, Etna Furnace played a crucial role in the early development of the region's iron industry, contributing to the economic growth of Southern Ohio during the 19th century. The furnace was strategically located to take advantage of the area's rich natural resources, including abundant iron ore, limestone, and timber, all of which were of vital importance.

Founders and Early Development

Thomas James, the founder of Etna Furnace, was a prominent figure in the early iron industry of Southern Ohio. Recognizing the potential of the region's natural resources, James established the furnace to meet the growing demand for iron products in the United States. The furnace was named "Etna" after Mount Etna, the famous volcano in Italy, symbolizing the fiery nature of the furnace's operations.

Etna Furnace was designed as a charcoal-fired blast furnace, a common design in the early 19th century. The furnace was constructed using locally sourced stone and was equipped with a large chimney stack to vent the gases produced during the smelting process. The location of the furnace was carefully chosen for its proximity to essential resources: iron ore was mined from nearby hills, timber for charcoal was harvested from the surrounding forests, and limestone was sourced locally to act as a flux in the process.

Operations and Workforce

Etna Furnace operated as a cold-blast furnace, using unheated air to aid in the smelting process. The furnace's operations were labor-intensive, requiring a large workforce to mine the iron ore, produce the charcoal, and operate the furnace. At its peak, Etna Furnace employed around 150 workers, making it one of the largest employers in the region at the time.

The workforce at Etna Furnace was composed of a mix of skilled and unskilled laborers, including furnace operators, colliers (charcoal burners), and general laborers, white and black. Many of the workers were immigrants from Europe, particularly Ireland and Germany, who brought valuable skills and experience to the furnace operations. Freed African-American slaves and other African-Americans commonly worked at this site and others. The workers lived in nearby company-owned housing, forming a close-knit community centered around the furnace.

The process of producing iron at Etna Furnace began with the mining of iron ore, which was transported to the furnace site. The ore was then combined with charcoal and limestone in the furnace stack, where it was heated to high temperatures to extract the iron. The molten iron was poured into molds to produce pig iron, which was then transported to markets via the Ohio River. The furnace operated continuously, with workers maintaining the furnace around the clock to ensure a steady supply of pig iron.

Economic Impact

Etna Furnace had a significant impact on the local economy, providing employment and supporting the development of infrastructure in Lawrence County. The success of the furnace attracted additional investment into the region, leading to the establishment of other iron furnaces and related industries. The iron produced at Etna Furnace was used in a variety of applications, including the construction of railroads, machinery, and tools, all of which were essential to the industrial growth of the United States.

The furnace also contributed to the development of transportation infrastructure in the region. Roads were built and maintained to facilitate the movement of raw materials and finished products, and the Ohio River served as a vital transportation route for shipping pig iron to markets in Cincinnati, Pittsburgh, and beyond.

Decline and Closure

As the 19th century progressed, Etna Furnace, like many other charcoal-fired furnaces in the region, began to face significant challenges. The depletion of local timber resources made charcoal production increasingly difficult and expensive. Additionally, the rise of coke-fired blast furnaces, which were more efficient and produced higher-quality iron, made the older charcoal furnaces less competitive.

Despite these challenges, Etna Furnace continued to operate for several decades, thanks to the resourcefulness of its operators and the dedication of its workforce. However, by the late 1880s, the furnace was no longer able to operate profitably. The furnace ceased operations, marking the end of an era for Lawrence County. The closure of Etna Furnace had a profound impact on the local community, leading to job losses and economic decline. Many of the workers who had depended on the furnace for their livelihood.

Legacy and Preservation

Today, the site of Etna Furnace is recognized as a historical landmark, with remnants of the furnace still visible in the landscape. Efforts have been made to preserve the site and educate the public about the furnace's history and its role in the development of the Hanging Rock Iron Region. Local historical societies and preservationists continue to research and document the history of Etna Furnace, ensuring that its legacy is remembered as part of Southern Ohio's industrial heritage.

The legacy of Etna Furnace is also reflected in the continued interest in the region's industrial history. The furnace's contribution to the early industrialization of the United States, as well as its impact on the local community, continues to be studied and celebrated by historians and preservationists. The site remains a testament to the hard work and ingenuity of the men and women who built and operated the furnace, and it serves as a reminder of the region's rich industrial past.

Modern Legacy

In addition to its historical significance, the site of Etna Furnace is part of a broader effort to preserve the industrial heritage of the Hanging Rock Iron Region. The furnace is one of several sites in the region that have been recognized for their importance in the history of American industry. Interpretive markers and educational programs help visitors understand the role that these furnaces played in the development of the United States and the impact they had on the lives of the people who lived here and elsewhere.

Etna Furnace's story is not just one of industrial success and decline, but also one of community and resilience. The furnace helped shape the social and economic fabric of Lawrence County, leaving a lasting legacy that continues to be felt in the region today. As such, Etna Furnace remains an important part of Southern Ohio's cultural and historical identity.

Etna Furnace's Company Town: A Thriving Community

Alongside the Etna Furnace, a vibrant company town emerged to support the workers and their families. The town was carefully planned and constructed to meet the needs of the growing community, with the Etna Iron Works investing heavily in housing and infrastructure.

In the early years of the town's development, the Etna Iron Works embarked on an ambitious construction project. They immediately built 45 cottages and four larger houses to accommodate the workers and their families. Additionally, they constructed a substantial brick storehouse and a warehouse measuring 24 by 80 feet, with an attached office. A large boarding house was also built to house single workers or those who had not yet brought their families to the town.

The company's commitment to the town's growth did not stop there. Plans were made to build an additional 40 houses in the near future, further expanding the community. The Etna Iron Works also invested in the town's economic diversification, with plans to establish a keg works facility and install machinery worth $40,000. This investment would create new job opportunities and support the town's long-term stability.

The town's lumber industry was also thriving, with a large sawmill in operation that employed 22 hands. The sawmill had secured contracts to deliver between 1,000,000 and 3,000,000 feet of lumber in monthly lots of 100,000 feet. Additionally, the sawmill had contracts for 2,000,000 shingles and 2,000,000 laths, reflecting the strong demand for building materials in the region.

Etna Furnace's company town was not only a place of industry but also a hub of social and cultural activity. The town's residents formed a close-knit community, supporting one another through the challenges of life in an industrial town. The company provided essential services, such as a general store, a school, and a church, which served as focal points for community life.

Etna Furnace and the Employment of Free Black Workers and Escaped Slaves

One unique aspect of Etna Furnace's workforce was the presence of free Black workers and escaped slaves. Unlike many other industrial operations of the time, Etna Furnace actively hired free Black laborers and provided employment opportunities for those who had escaped from slavery.

The decision to employ free Black workers and escaped slaves was a progressive one for the era, reflecting a commitment to providing opportunities for those who had been marginalized and oppressed. By offering employment and a measure of security, Etna Furnace became a beacon of hope for many African Americans seeking to build new lives in freedom.

The presence of free Black workers and escaped slaves in the company town added to the diversity and richness of the community. These individuals brought with them their own experiences, skills, and cultural traditions, contributing to the vibrant tapestry of life in the town.

However, the employment of free Black workers and escaped slaves was not without its challenges. The fugitive slave laws of the time meant that those who had escaped from slavery were constantly at risk of being captured and returned to their enslavers. The management and workers at Etna Furnace had to navigate these legal and social challenges while providing a safe and supportive environment for their African American employees.

Despite these challenges, the presence of free Black workers and escaped slaves at Etna Furnace stands as a testament to the resilience and determination of those who sought to build new lives in the face of adversity. Their stories, though often untold, are an essential part of the history of the furnace and its company town.

Today, the legacy of Etna Furnace's inclusive employment practices serves as a reminder of the complex social and racial dynamics of the 19th century and the ongoing struggle for equality and opportunity that has shaped the nation's history. As we examine the industrial heritage of Southern Ohio, it is crucial to recognize the contributions and experiences of all those who lived and worked in these communities, regardless of their background or social status.

Etna Furnace's company town was a vibrant and dynamic community that supported the furnace's operations and provided a home for hundreds of workers and their families, including free Black laborers and escaped slaves. The town's growth and development were a testament to the economic and social importance of the iron industry in the Hanging Rock Iron Region.

The employment of free Black workers and escaped slaves at Etna Furnace adds a significant dimension to the site's history, highlighting the complex social and racial realities of the era. As we explore the industrial heritage of Southern Ohio, it is essential to recognize the diverse experiences and contributions of all those who lived and worked in these communities.

Today, the legacy of Etna Furnace and its company town lives on through the efforts of local historians, preservationists, and community members who work to preserve and interpret this important piece of regional history. By engaging with this history, we gain a deeper understanding of the forces that shaped the development of Southern Ohio and the broader story of American industrialization.

Chapter 18

Hearths and Homes: Life in the Iron Furnace Company Towns

Housing and life: Living Within The Rural Appalachian Foothills

Life in the Company Towns: Housing, Chores, and Daily Routines

Water Retrieval and Usage

One of the most crucial and time-consuming tasks in the company towns was the retrieval and management of water. Without running water or indoor plumbing, families had to rely on nearby water sources, such as wells, springs, or streams, to meet their daily needs. The distance to these water sources varied depending on the location of the house and the layout of the town, but it was not uncommon for families to walk a quarter mile to half a mile or more each way to fetch water.

The task of water retrieval often fell to the women and children of the household, as the men were typically engaged in long shifts at the iron furnace. Women would wake up early, often before sunrise, to begin their daily chores, which started with fetching water. They would grab wooden buckets, yokes, or large jugs and set off on foot to the nearest water source.

Wooden buckets were the most common vessels used for water retrieval. These buckets were typically made from readily available materials such as oak, pine, or cedar and were constructed by local craftsmen or coopers. The buckets featured a wooden handle and metal hoops to reinforce the structure. A typical bucket could hold around 2-3 gallons of water, weighing approximately 16-24 pounds when full.

For larger quantities of water, women might use a yoke, a wooden beam with a hook or a bucket at each end, which allowed them to carry two buckets at once, distributing the weight evenly across their shoulders. This method enabled them to transport up to 4-6 gallons of water per trip, although it required significant strength and endurance.

The number of trips and the total amount of water collected each day depended on the size of the family and their specific needs. A family of six might on certain days require around 30-40 gallons of water per day for drinking, cooking, cleaning, and washing. This could mean 15-20 trips to the water source, with each trip taking 30-40 minutes or more, depending on the distance and terrain. In total, a woman on a busy day may have spent 6-8 hours or more each day just on water retrieval!

Once the water was brought back to the house, it would be poured into larger storage containers, such as barrels or cisterns, which were typically located near the kitchen or the back porch. These containers were made from wood, ceramics, or metal and could hold anywhere from 10 to 50 gallons of water. The water would be ladled out as needed for various tasks throughout the day, such as cooking, cleaning, and washing.

In some cases, families might have access to a well located closer to their home, either on their property or shared with neighboring houses. These wells were typically dug by hand, often by the men of the community, and lined with stone or brick to prevent collapse. A well could range from 10 to 50 feet deep, depending on the depth of the water table, and would be equipped with a bucket and rope or a hand pump to draw the water up.

While a well could provide a more convenient source of water, it still required significant labor to operate and maintain. The well would need to be regularly cleaned and repaired, and the water would still need to be carried into the house for use. In times of drought or low water levels, a well might run dry, forcing families to seek alternative sources or to ration their water use carefully.

The constant need for water and the physical labor involved in its retrieval had a profound impact on the daily lives of women in the company towns. The time and energy spent on this single task limited their ability to engage in other activities, such as childcare, gardening, or social interaction. It also took a toll on their physical health, leading to chronic pain, injuries, and exhaustion.

Despite these challenges, women in the company towns developed a range of strategies and skills to manage their water needs effectively. They would often coordinate their water retrieval with other chores, such as washing clothes or gathering firewood, to minimize the number of trips needed. They would also develop a keen understanding of the water sources in their area, knowing which ones were the most reliable or the easiest to access in different seasons.

The communal nature of water retrieval also fostered a sense of solidarity and support among the women of the company towns. They would often walk to the water source together, using the time to socialize, share news and advice, and commiserate about the challenges of their daily lives. This shared experience helped to build a strong sense of community and resilience in the face of hardship.

Sanitation and Outhouses

Proper sanitation was a constant challenge in the company towns, with the lack of indoor plumbing and the reliance on outhouses or privies for waste disposal. These simple structures, typically built of wood and located a short distance from the main house, consisted of a small room with one or more seats over a deep pit.

The outhouses in the company towns were usually basic in design, with a wooden frame, a sloped roof, and a door for privacy. The seats were often made of wood, with one or more holes cut into them to allow waste to fall into the pit below. Some outhouses might have a small window for ventilation, while others relied on gaps in the walls or door for air flow.

The pits beneath the outhouses were typically dug by hand, often by the men of the household or community. They would range from 3 to 6 feet deep and were sometimes lined with stone or brick to prevent collapse. When a pit became full, it would be covered with soil, and a new pit would be dug nearby to replace it.

Outhouses were usually located a short distance from the main house, typically around 50 to 100 feet away, to minimize odors and the risk of contamination. They were often situated downwind from the house and away from any water sources to prevent pollution.

The use of outhouses required regular maintenance and cleaning to keep them functional and hygienic. This task often fell to the women of the household, who would scrub the seats and floors with homemade soap and water, and sprinkle lime or wood ashes into the pit to control odors and aid in decomposition.

In the winter months, using the outhouse could be a particularly unpleasant experience, with the cold temperatures and the need to navigate through snow or mud to reach the structure. Some families might use chamber pots or bedpans during the coldest months to avoid the trek to the outhouse, but these still needed to be emptied and cleaned regularly.

The lack of proper sanitation in the company towns posed significant health risks, particularly in terms of waterborne diseases such as cholera, typhoid, and dysentery. The close proximity of outhouses to water sources, combined with the lack of understanding about the spread of disease, meant that contamination was a constant threat. As a result, outbreaks of illness were common in the company towns, particularly during the summer months when warmer temperatures accelerated the spread of bacteria. Children and the elderly were particularly vulnerable, with high rates of infant mortality and shortened life expectancies.

Despite these risks, the use of outhouses remained the primary means of waste disposal in the company towns well into the 20th century. The cost and complexity of installing indoor plumbing, combined with the isolation and limited resources of many towns, meant that the transition to modern sanitation was slow and uneven.

In some cases, the company towns would eventually install communal privies or latrines, which were larger structures with multiple seats that could serve several families at once. These were typically located near the center of town and were maintained by the company or the community as a whole.

The legacy of the outhouses in the company towns can still be seen today, with many of the original structures still standing in various states of disrepair. Some have been preserved as historical artifacts, offering a glimpse into the daily lives and challenges of the people who once used them.

One notable figure in the history of outhouses is Charles "Chic" Sale, an American actor, writer, and comedian who was born in Huron, South Dakota in 1885. Sale became famous in the early 20th century for his humorous sketches and books, many of which revolved around the theme of outhouses and rural life. Sale's most famous work was "The Specialist," a comedic monologue that was first published in 1929 and later adapted into a short film. The monologue tells the story of Lem Putt, a fictional carpenter who specializes in building outhouses. Through Lem's voice, Sale offers a humorous and satirical take on the design, construction, and use of outhouses, poking fun at the social customs and taboos surrounding the topic. The popularity of "The Specialist" helped to cement Sale's reputation as a comedic writer and performer, and also contributed to the growing cultural fascination with outhouses as a symbol of rural Americana. Sale's work played a significant role in shaping public perceptions of outhouses and in preserving their legacy as an important part of the country's social and architectural history.

Today, the term "chic sale" is still used in some parts of this part of Appalachia as a slang term for an outhouse, a testament to the enduring impact of Sale's work on American popular culture. The humble outhouse, once a ubiquitous feature of daily life in the company towns and rural communities across the country, has become a symbol of a bygone era and a reminder of the challenges and resilience of the people who once relied on them.

Soap Making and Cleaning

Cleanliness was a constant challenge in the company towns, with the omnipresent soot and grime from the iron furnaces and the lack of running water. To keep their homes and families clean, women had to rely on homemade soap and labor-intensive washing methods.

Soap making was a common household chore, typically done once or twice a year in large batches. The process involved combining animal fat, such as lard or tallow, with lye, a caustic substance derived from wood ashes. The exact recipe and method for soap making varied, but a typical process would involve the following steps:

1. Collecting and storing wood ashes in a wooden barrel or hopper throughout the year. Hardwood ashes, such as those from oak or hickory, were preferred for their higher potassium content. The ashes would be saved from the fireplace or stove and stored in a dry place until enough had accumulated to make a batch of soap.

2. Making the lye solution by pouring water through the ashes and collecting the resulting liquid, which would be rich in potassium hydroxide. This process was known as leaching and could take several days. The lye solution would be collected in a wooden barrel or crock and then tested for strength using a raw egg or a feather. If the egg floated or the feather dissolved, the lye was strong enough for soap making.
3. Rendering animal fat by boiling it in a large iron kettle until it melted and any impurities had risen to the surface. The fat would be collected throughout the year from cooking, butchering, or other sources and stored in a cool place until soap making time. Lard (pork fat) or tallow (beef fat) were the most common types used, but other fats such as goose grease or bear oil could also be used.
4. Combining the lye solution and the rendered fat in a specific ratio, typically around 1 part lye to 6-8 parts fat, and stirring the mixture continuously over low heat until it began to thicken. This process could take several hours and required constant attention to prevent the mixture from separating or burning. The temperature of the mixture had to be carefully controlled, as too much heat could cause the soap to become brittle or crumbly.
5. Adding any desired fragrances or additives, such as essential oils or herbs, to the soap mixture. These ingredients were often gathered from the family's garden or purchased from the company store or traveling peddlers. Common additives included lavender, rosemary, peppermint, or lemon balm, which were believed to have beneficial properties for the skin or to mask the strong odor of the lye.
6. Pouring the soap into wooden molds and allowing it to cool and harden for several days or weeks. The molds were typically simple wooden boxes lined with cloth or paper, which could be easily removed once the soap had set. The size and shape of the molds varied, but a common size was a rectangular block around 3-4 inches thick and 12-18 inches long, which could be cut into smaller bars as needed.
7. Cutting the soap into bars and storing it in a cool, dry place until needed. The bars would be cut using a wire or string and then stacked on shelves or in a basket to cure for several weeks or months. During this time, the soap would continue to harden and dry out, making it more effective for cleaning and longer-lasting.

This homemade soap, while crude by modern standards, was effective in cleaning clothes, dishes, and even the body. Women would use the soap to scrub clothing on washboards or in large wooden tubs, often using boiling water to help loosen the dirt and stains. The clothes would then be rinsed in clean water, wrung out, and hung on lines or bushes to dry in the sun.

For personal hygiene, families would typically bathe once a week, using a large wooden tub filled with water heated on the stove or over the fireplace. The soap would be used to scrub the body, and the water would be shared among family members, with the oldest bathing first and the youngest last. In between baths, family members would use a washcloth and basin to clean their faces, hands, and feet daily.

The making and use of soap were deeply ingrained in the daily lives of women in the company towns. It was a task that required skill, knowledge, and patience, passed down from mother to daughter and shared among neighbors. The harsh lye and animal fats could be damaging to the skin, leading to dryness, cracking, and irritation. Women would often use homemade salves or lotions made from beeswax, herbs, or oils to soothe and protect their hands.

Despite the challenges, soap making was also a source of pride and creativity for many women. They would experiment with different ingredients and techniques to create soaps that were both functional and pleasant to use. Some would add colors or patterns to their soaps using natural dyes or molds, creating small works of art that could be traded or given as gifts.

The importance of soap making in the company towns cannot be overstated. It was a critical component of daily hygiene and sanitation, helping to prevent the spread of disease and maintain the health of the community. It was also a reflection of the self-sufficiency and resourcefulness of the women who lived there, who had to make do with limited resources and rely on their own skills and knowledge to keep their families clean and healthy.

Lighting and Fuel

In the absence of electricity, families in the company towns relied on a variety of methods for lighting their homes. The primary sources of light were candles, oil lamps, and lanterns, each with its own specific fuel and method of operation.

Candles were a common and relatively inexpensive form of lighting, often made at home using tallow (rendered animal fat) or beeswax. To make candles, the tallow would be melted in a large iron kettle and then poured into candle molds, which were typically made of tin or pewter. A cotton wick would be suspended in the center of each mold, and the melted tallow would be poured around it. Once cooled and hardened, the candles would be removed from the molds, trimmed, and stored for use.

Candle molds were often passed down through generations or purchased from local craftsmen or the company store. Some families also used dipped candles, which were made by repeatedly dipping a wick into melted tallow until the desired thickness was achieved.

The tallow used for candle making would be collected throughout the year from the butchering of animals, primarily cows and sheep. The fat would be cut into small pieces and then boiled in a large kettle until it had melted and any impurities had risen to the surface. The liquid tallow would then be strained through a cloth and poured into molds or saved for later use.

Beeswax candles were also used in the company towns, although they were more expensive and harder to obtain than tallow candles. Beeswax was collected from honey bee hives and then melted and strained to remove impurities. It had a higher melting point than tallow, making it more suitable for use in the summer months, and it also burned brighter and cleaner than tallow candles.

Oil lamps were another common form of lighting, using various fuels such as whale oil, lard oil, or kerosene. These lamps consisted of a glass or metal reservoir to hold the fuel, a wick to draw the fuel up, and a mechanism to adjust the height of the wick and control the brightness of the flame.

The most common type of oil lamp in the mid-19th century was the "burning fluid" lamp, which used a mixture of turpentine and alcohol as fuel. These lamps provided a brighter and cleaner-burning light than candles, but they were also more expensive and required regular maintenance, such as trimming the wick and refilling the reservoir.

Kerosene lamps, introduced in the 1850s, became increasingly popular in the later years of the company towns. Kerosene, a distilled product of petroleum, was cheaper and more readily available than other lamp fuels. It also burned brighter and cleaner than earlier fuels. Kerosene lamps featured a glass chimney to protect the flame and improve air flow, and a wick adjustment mechanism to control the brightness.

Lanterns were portable lighting devices that used candles or oil lamps as their light source. They were made of metal or glass and featured a protective hood or globe to shield the flame from wind and rain. Lanterns were particularly useful for outdoor work or for moving between buildings at night.

The fuel for these lighting devices, whether it be tallow, oil, or kerosene, was typically purchased from the company store or from traveling peddlers who visited the towns. Whale oil, lard oil, and kerosene were shipped in barrels from coastal whaling stations, rendering plants, or oil refineries and then distributed to local stores by wagon or riverboat. The barrels of fuel would be delivered to the company store by horse-drawn wagons or, in some cases, by rail. The store owner would then dispense the fuel into smaller containers, such as tin cans or glass bottles, for purchase by individual families. The price of the fuel would be added to the family's account at the store, to be paid off with future wages from the iron furnace.

The amount of fuel used and the duration of lighting depended on the specific needs of each family and the availability of resources. A typical family might use 1-2 gallons of kerosene per week for lighting, with each gallon providing around 40-50 hours of burn time in a kerosene lamp.

Heating and Cooking

Heating and cooking in the company towns revolved around the fireplace or the stove, both of which required a steady supply of fuel in the form of wood or coal. The specific type of fuel used depended on the location of the town and the availability of resources.

In towns situated near the iron furnaces or in heavily forested areas, wood was the primary fuel source. Men and older boys would be responsible for chopping and collecting firewood from the surrounding forests, using axes and hand saws to fell trees and split the logs into manageable pieces. The wood would be stacked in a woodshed or pile near the house to dry and season, a process that could take several months.

A typical family might use 10-20 cords of wood per year for heating and cooking, with a cord being a stack of wood measuring 4 feet high, 4 feet wide, and 8 feet long. This would require a significant amount of time and labor to harvest, transport, and store the wood.

In towns located near coal seams or with access to coal through the company store, coal was often used as a supplementary or alternative fuel source. Coal, a dense, carbon-rich rock formed from the remains of ancient plants, burned hotter and longer than wood and was particularly useful for iron stoves or furnaces.

Coal was typically mined from local seams by the iron company or independent miners and then transported to the town by wagon or rail. Families would purchase coal by the bushel or ton from the company store and store it in a coal shed or bin near the house.

The fireplace or stove was the heart of the home, providing both heat and a means of cooking. Fireplaces were typically made of stone or brick and featured a large, open hearth for burning wood. The fireplace would be lit in the morning to warm the house and provide a source of light and heat for cooking throughout the day. Cooking over the fireplace involved the use of cast iron pots, kettles, and skillets, which would be suspended over the fire on iron cranes or tripods. Women would prepare meals such as stews, soups, and porridges in large pots, while meats and vegetables would be roasted on spits or in Dutch ovens placed directly on the coals.

The design and construction of fireplaces varied depending on the resources available and the skills of the local masons and bricklayers. In some cases, fireplaces would be built using local stone, such as sandstone or limestone, which would be cut and shaped into blocks and then mortared together to form the hearth and chimney. In other cases, bricks would be used, either purchased from a local brickyard or made on-site using clay from the surrounding area.

The building of a fireplace was a skilled trade that required knowledge of materials, construction techniques, and fire safety. Masons would need to ensure that the fireplace was properly vented to allow smoke to escape and that the hearth was large enough to contain the fire and prevent sparks from igniting the surrounding woodwork. They would also need to build the chimney to the proper height to create sufficient draft and prevent back-smoking into the room.

The origins of the fireplace can be traced back to the earliest human dwellings, where an open fire would be built in the center of the room to provide heat, light, and a means of cooking. Over time, the fireplace evolved to become a more permanent and efficient structure, with the addition of a hearth, chimney, and various tools and accessories for managing the fire and cooking food.

In colonial America, the fireplace was a central feature of the home, serving as a gathering place for the family and a symbol of domestic life. The design and decoration of the fireplace often reflected the wealth and status of the homeowner, with more elaborate mantels, tiles, and ironwork used in the homes of the affluent.

As technology advanced, iron stoves began to replace the open fireplace as a more efficient and convenient means of heating and cooking. These stoves, which burned either wood or coal, provided a more controllable and consistent heat source and allowed for a greater variety of cooking techniques, such as baking and roasting.

The first iron stoves appeared in Europe in the early 18th century and were introduced to America by German settlers in Pennsylvania. These early stoves were simple, box-like structures made of cast iron, with a single door for loading fuel and a few holes on the top for pots and pans. Over time, stove designs became more elaborate, with the addition of ovens, warming drawers, and decorative features such as nickel-plated trim and enamel finishes.

In the company towns of the Hanging Rock Iron Region, iron stoves were a common sight, often purchased from the company store or ordered from manufacturers in nearby cities such as Cincinnati or Pittsburgh. These stoves were typically made of cast iron, with a main compartment for burning fuel, an oven for baking, and a series of burners or eyes on the top for cooking.

The most popular stove brands in the mid-19th century included the "Buck's Stove," named after its inventor, William Buck, and the "Charter Oak Stove," manufactured by the Excelsior Manufacturing

Company of St. Louis, Missouri. These stoves were known for their durability, efficiency, and innovative features, such as the "patent oven regulator," which allowed for more precise temperature control.

Despite the advantages of iron stoves, many families in the company towns continued to rely on the open fireplace for cooking and heating, particularly in the early years of settlement. The transition to stoves was gradual, with some households using both methods depending on the season and the type of food being prepared.

The skills and techniques of cooking over an open fire were passed down from generation to generation, with women learning from their mothers and grandmothers how to manage the flames, control the heat, and cook a variety of dishes using simple tools and ingredients. These skills were essential for survival in the harsh conditions of the company towns, where access to fresh food and supplies was often limited.

Food and Cooking

Food preparation and cooking were constant chores in the company towns, with women spending a significant portion of their day tending to the needs of their families. The specific foods and cooking methods varied depending on the season, the availability of ingredients, and the cultural background of the family, but there were some common staples and techniques.

One of the most important factors in determining the diet of company town families was the availability of food. Most families relied on a combination of store-bought goods, locally grown produce, and wild game or fish to feed themselves.

Certain shelf-stable items such as flour, sugar, salt, coffee, and dried beans were purchased from the company store in large quantities. These goods were shipped to the store by steamboat or rail from wholesale merchants in larger cities and then sold to families on credit, with the cost deducted from the miners' wages.

Perishable items such as fresh produce, dairy, and meat were more difficult to obtain and store in the company towns. Some families had small gardens where they could grow vegetables and herbs, while others relied on local farmers or the company store's limited selection. Meat was often preserved through smoking, salting, or canning, as fresh meat was a rare luxury.

Wild game and fish provided an important supplement to the diets of many families. Men and boys would hunt for squirrels, rabbits, deer, and other game in the surrounding forests, while fish could be caught in nearby streams and rivers. These wild foods added variety and nutrition to the often monotonous diet of store-bought staples.

The preparation and cooking of meals was a time-consuming and labor-intensive process, typically done by the women of the household. Breakfast was often the most substantial meal of the day, as it fueled the men for their long shifts in the mines. A typical breakfast might include fried potatoes, ham or bacon, biscuits or cornbread, and coffee or tea.

Dinner, served in the early afternoon, was usually a one-pot meal such as a stew, soup, or beans, accompanied by cornbread or biscuits. These dishes could be left to simmer on the stove or over the fire while the women attended to other chores, and they made use of whatever ingredients were available, including vegetables from the garden, wild game, or leftover meats.

Supper, served in the evening, was a lighter meal and might consist of leftovers from dinner, bread and butter, or a simple dish such as fried potatoes or cornbread with molasses.

Women would also be responsible for baking bread, which was a staple of the company town diet. Cornbread, made from cornmeal, was the most common type of bread, as it was cheap and easy to make. Biscuits, made from flour, lard, and milk or buttermilk, were also popular and could be made quickly on the stovetop or in a Dutch oven.

Canning and preserving were important skills for women in the company towns, as they allowed foods to be stored for the winter months when fresh produce was scarce. Fruits and vegetables from the garden or from wild sources, such as berries and nuts, would be preserved through canning, drying, or pickling. Meats could also be canned or smoked to extend their shelf life.

The company store was the primary source of the ingredients and tools needed for food preparation and cooking. Flour, cornmeal, sugar, and other staples were purchased in bulk and then used to make bread, cakes, pies, and other baked goods. Lard, used for frying and baking, was rendered from pork fat and could be bought at the store or made at home.

Coffee and tea were luxury items that were highly prized by company town families. Coffee was typically bought green and then roasted and ground at home, while tea was purchased in loose-leaf form and brewed in a teapot or kettle. These beverages were often served with meals or enjoyed as a special treat.

Cooking tools and equipment were also purchased from the company store or from traveling peddlers. Cast iron pots, skillets, and Dutch ovens were essential for cooking over an open fire, while tin or copper kettles were used for boiling water and making soups and stews. Wooden spoons, ladles, and other utensils were carved by hand or bought from local craftsmen.

Despite the challenges of limited ingredients and primitive cooking methods, the women of the company towns developed a rich culinary tradition that made use of the resources available to them. Recipes and techniques were passed down from mother to daughter, and women would often share their knowledge and skills with each other through informal networks of friends and neighbors.

Some common dishes that were popular in the company towns included:

1. Cornbread and beans: A simple but hearty meal made from cornmeal, water, and salt, served with a side of boiled beans seasoned with pork fat or ham hocks.
2. Fried potatoes: Potatoes were a cheap and filling staple that could be fried in lard or bacon grease and served as a side dish or a main course.
3. Soup beans: A thick, creamy soup made from dried beans, onions, and pork or bacon, often served with cornbread or biscuits.
4. Squirrel stew: A savory stew made from wild squirrel meat, vegetables, and spices, simmered for hours until tender.
5. Apple stack cake: A special occasion dessert made from layers of thin, spiced cake, spread with a filling of stewed apples and spices, and stacked high.

These dishes, along with many others, formed the basis of the company town diet and reflected the resourcefulness and creativity of the women who prepared them. They were simple, hearty, and made use of the ingredients that were available, but they also held deep cultural and emotional significance for the families who ate them.

Daily Life and Chores

Life in the company towns was shaped by the demands of the iron industry and the need to maintain the household. Men, women, and children all had specific roles and responsibilities that contributed to the family's survival and well-being.

For men, the workday began early, often before sunrise. They would rise, eat a quick breakfast of cornbread or biscuits with coffee or tea, and then head off to the iron furnace for a long shift of 12 hours or more. The work at the furnace was grueling and dangerous, involving the handling of heavy machinery, molten iron, and intense heat.

The men would typically work six days a week, with Sundays off for rest and religious observance. The exception to this was during times of high demand or "blows," when the furnace would operate continuously for days or even weeks at a time. During these blows, the men would work in shifts around the clock, snatching a few hours of sleep when they could in the sheds or shanties near the furnace.

Despite the harsh conditions, many men took pride in their work at the furnace, seeing it as a source of steady employment and a means of providing for their families. They developed a strong sense of camaraderie with their fellow workers, often forming close-knit bonds that extended beyond the workplace.

For women, the workday was no less demanding, though it revolved around the endless tasks of maintaining the household and caring for the family. Women would rise early to stoke the fire, prepare breakfast, and get the children ready for the day.

They would then spend much of the day engaged in a variety of chores, including:

1. Cleaning: Sweeping, dusting, and scrubbing the floors, furniture, and windows to keep the house clean and tidy. This was a constant battle against the soot and grime that would blow in from the furnace and settle on every surface.
2. Laundry: Washing and ironing clothes, bedding, and other linens using homemade soap, a washboard, and a bucket or tub. The clothes would be boiled in a large kettle over the fire,

then scrubbed, rinsed, and wrung out by hand before being hung to dry on a line or laid flat on bushes.
3. Sewing and mending: Making and repairing clothes, curtains, and other household textiles using a needle and thread, or a hand-cranked sewing machine if they were lucky enough to have one. Women would often make clothes for the whole family out of flour sacks, feed bags, or other repurposed materials.
4. Gardening and food preservation: Planting, tending, and harvesting a kitchen garden to provide fresh vegetables and herbs for the family. Women would also preserve food for the winter by canning, pickling, or drying fruits and vegetables, and by making jams, jellies, and other preserves.
5. Child care and education: Caring for infants and young children, nursing them, changing diapers, and teaching them the skills and values they would need to survive in the world. Women would also often take on the role of educating the children, teaching them to read, write, and do basic arithmetic, as well as passing on the cultural traditions and folklore of the community.

In addition to these daily chores, women would also be responsible for managing the household finances, budgeting the family's income and expenses, and making sure they had enough food and supplies to last the week or the month. This was a challenging task in the company towns, where wages were often low and unpredictable, and where the cost of goods at the company store was often inflated.

For children, life in the company towns was a mix of work, play, and education. From a young age, children were expected to contribute to the household by helping with chores, tending to younger siblings, and even working in the iron furnace or coal mines if they were old enough.

Boys as young as 10 or 12 might be hired to work as "breaker boys," sorting coal by hand and removing impurities, or as "trappers," opening and closing the doors of the mine to allow coal cars to pass through. Girls might be sent to work in the company store or in the homes of wealthier families as domestic servants.

Despite the demands of work and household chores, children in the company towns still found time for play and socializing. They would often gather in the streets or the woods to play games, tell stories, and explore the natural world around them. Popular games included marbles, hopscotch, and tag, as well as more rough-and-tumble activities like wrestling and tree climbing.

Education for children in the company towns was often limited, with many families unable to afford the time or money to send their children to school regularly. Some company towns had their own schools, which were typically one-room schoolhouses that served children of all ages. These schools were often underfunded and understaffed, with a single teacher responsible for teaching all subjects.

Chapter 19

Iron's Eternal Echo: The Lasting Legacy of The Hanging Rock Iron Region

Echos In The Hollers

As the sun sets over the rolling hills of southern Ohio, northern Kentucky, and western West Virginia, its golden rays catch the weathered stones of long-silent iron furnaces. These sentinels of a bygone era stand as testaments to the dreams, struggles, and triumphs of generations past. In the quiet of twilight, one can almost hear the echoes of hammers striking iron, the hiss of molten metal, and the voices of those who once called this place home. This is the Hanging Rock Iron Region, a land where the story of America's industrial awakening is written not just in history books, but in the very earth itself.

Our journey through the annals of this remarkable region has been more than a mere recounting of dates and facts. It has been a pilgrimage into the heart of a community forged as surely as the iron that flowed from its furnaces. From the early pioneers who first recognized the potential hidden within these hills to the last workers who watched the fires die out, each person who lived and labored here has left an indelible mark on the tapestry of this land.

The iron furnaces that once stood proud against the sky, belching smoke and fire, now stand in quiet dignity amidst a landscape that has begun to soften their harsh lines. Where once the ground was stripped bare to fuel the insatiable appetite of industry, now trees reach skyward, their roots entwining with the foundations of abandoned structures. Wildflowers peek through cracks in old stone walls, and birdsong has replaced the clamor of machinery. It's as if the land itself is reclaiming its children, welcoming them back into its embrace after their long sojourn in the world of human endeavor.

This gradual return to nature is not an erasure of history, but rather a poignant reminder of the cyclical nature of all things. The iron ore that was pulled from the earth, the trees that were felled for charcoal, the limestone quarried for flux - all these elements are slowly but surely finding their way back to their origins. In this gentle reclamation, we see a powerful metaphor for the resilience of both nature and the human spirit.

The story of the Hanging Rock Iron Region is, at its core, a human story. It's a tale of men and women who came from far and wide, drawn by the promise of work and the hope of a better life. They brought with them diverse backgrounds, languages, and customs, yet in the shadow of the furnaces, they forged a community as strong as the iron they produced.

Consider the life of Samuel Thompson, a freed slave who found work at the Olive Furnace in the years following the Civil War. Thompson's calloused hands and unflagging spirit helped build not just an industry, but a future for his family. His granddaughter, Mary, would go on to become one of the first African American teachers in Lawrence County, her achievements a testament to the opportunities her grandfather's labor had secured. Or think of Katerina Novak, who arrived from Bohemia in 1870 with little more than the clothes on her back and a fierce determination to succeed. In the company town of Union Furnace, she found not just employment as a laundress, but a community that embraced her. Her pierogies became legendary among the furnace workers, a taste of home in a foreign land, and a symbol of the cultural tapestry that the iron industry helped weave.

These personal stories, multiplied a thousandfold, form the true legacy of the Hanging Rock Iron Region. They remind us that behind every ton of iron produced, every rail laid, and every building erected, there were individuals with hopes, dreams, and fears. They faced backbreaking labor, dangerous working conditions, and an uncertain future with a courage that we can only marvel at today.

The company towns that grew up around the furnaces were more than just places to live - they were crucibles of community, where the bonds of shared experience forged relationships as strong as any family tie. In these towns, neighbors looked out for one another, sharing what little they had in times of hardship. Children played in the streets, their laughter a counterpoint to the constant rumble of the furnaces. Women gathered at well pumps and over wash lines, sharing news and advice, their conversations the lifeblood of the community.

It was in these towns that the true spirit of the Hanging Rock Iron Region was born - a spirit of resilience, mutual support, and unwavering determination. This spirit survived long after the last furnace went cold, passed down through generations like a precious heirloom. Today, you can still see it in the eyes of the descendants of those iron workers, hear it in the stories told around kitchen tables and at local gatherings.

The iron produced in this region quite literally helped build a nation. From the rails that connected coast to coast, to the beams that reached for the sky in America's burgeoning cities, to the plows that tamed the western prairies - Hanging Rock iron was there. It's a legacy written in steel and stone, a tangible reminder of the region's contribution to the American story.

But perhaps the most valuable product of the Hanging Rock Iron Region was not iron at all, but rather the intangible qualities forged in its furnaces - grit, determination, innovation, and community. These are the true treasures that have been passed down through generations, shaping the character of the region and its people long after the last ingot was poured.

As we stand today amidst the quiet ruins of once-mighty furnaces, we are reminded of the impermanence of human endeavors and the enduring power of nature. The same hills that once gave up their bounty of ore and timber now cradle the remnants of industry in a gentle embrace of vegetation. Moss creeps over old stone foundations, and trees push through the floors of abandoned buildings, their branches reaching for the sky just as the smokestacks once did.

This gradual reclamation by nature is not an ending, but a continuation of a cycle as old as the earth itself. It speaks to the resilience of the natural world and offers a powerful lesson in adaptation and renewal. Just as the land has found new life amidst the ruins of industry, so too have the communities of the Hanging Rock Iron Region reinvented themselves in the face of changing economic realities.

Today, efforts to preserve and interpret the history of the Hanging Rock Iron Region are ongoing, driven by a deep respect for the achievements of the past and a recognition of their relevance to the present. Museums, historical societies, and community groups work tirelessly to ensure that the stories of the iron furnaces and the people who operated them are not lost to time.

The Hanging Rock Region Today

As the sun rises over the rolling hills of southern Ohio, northern Kentucky, and western West Virginia, it illuminates a landscape that bears the indelible marks of its industrial past. The Hanging Rock Iron Region, once a bustling hub of iron production, now stands as a living museum of America's industrial heritage. In this chapter, we explore how the remnants of this bygone era have fared in the modern world, from crumbling ruins hidden in dense forests to carefully preserved historical sites that attract tourists from across the country.

Hidden Treasures in the Forest

Many of the once-mighty furnaces that dotted the Hanging Rock landscape have been reclaimed by nature. Deep in the forests of Wayne National Forest and surrounding areas, keen-eyed hikers and history enthusiasts can stumble upon the remnants of these industrial giants.

The Vesuvius Furnace, once one of the largest in the region, now stands as a silent sentinel in a clearing of the Wayne National Forest. Its massive stone stack, partially covered in moss and vines, looms over visitors, offering a tangible connection to the past. The furnace's current state of preservation is due in part to its remote location, which has protected it from vandalism and development.

Similarly, the remains of Olive Furnace can be found off the beaten path in Lawrence County. While much of the structure has crumbled over time, the base of the furnace and parts of the casting house still stand, providing a haunting glimpse into the scale of these operations. Local hiking groups occasionally organize guided tours to these hidden sites, combining outdoor recreation with historical education.

Preserved Sites and Living History

Not all of the Hanging Rock Iron Region's furnaces have been lost to time. Several sites have been carefully preserved and developed into educational attractions that offer visitors a glimpse into the region's industrial past.

The Buckeye Furnace State Memorial in Jackson County is perhaps the best-preserved example of a 19th-century charcoal iron furnace in the region. Restored to its 1860s appearance, the site includes the furnace, casting house, and company store. Living history demonstrations during summer months bring the site to life, with costumed interpreters demonstrating iron-making techniques and discussing daily life in the furnace community.

In Scioto County, the remains of Scioto Furnace have been incorporated into a small park. While not as extensively restored as

Buckeye Furnace, interpretive signs provide information about the site's history and importance to the local community. The park serves as a popular picnic spot for locals and a point of interest for passing tourists.

Towns Transformed

The company towns that once supported these furnaces have undergone significant transformations over the past century. Some have disappeared entirely, while others have evolved to meet the changing needs of their communities.

Hanging Rock, Ohio, which lent its name to the entire iron region, is a prime example of a former iron town that has adapted to the modern era. While iron production no longer drives the local economy, the town has preserved much of its 19th-century architecture. The former company store now houses a museum dedicated to the area's iron-making history, featuring artifacts, photographs, and personal accounts from former iron workers and their descendants.

In contrast, the town of Ironton, once home to several iron furnaces, has diversified its economy while still honoring its industrial heritage. The Ironton River Walk features interpretive displays about the town's iron-making past, integrated with modern recreational facilities. The annual Ironton-Lawrence County Memorial Day Parade, one of the oldest continuous Memorial Day parades in the nation, pays homage to the area's industrial and military history.

Tourism and Economic Impact

The preservation and promotion of the Hanging Rock Iron Region's industrial heritage have become important components of the area's tourism strategy. The Ohio Department of Natural Resources and local historical societies have worked together to create the Hanging Rock Iron Region Heritage Trail, a self-guided tour that takes visitors to key sites across southern Ohio.

This focus on industrial heritage tourism has provided a modest but significant boost to local economies. Small businesses catering to tourists, such as bed and breakfasts, cafes, and souvenir shops, have sprung up in towns along the heritage trail. Annual events, like the

Hanging Rock Iron Festival in Pedro, Ohio, draw thousands of visitors, celebrating the region's history with reenactments, craft demonstrations, and local food vendors.

Challenges and Opportunities

Despite these successes, the preservation of the Hanging Rock Iron Region's heritage faces ongoing challenges. Limited funding for maintenance and restoration of historical sites is a constant concern. Additionally, as generations pass, there is a risk of losing the personal connections and oral histories that bring these sites to life.

However, new technologies are opening up opportunities for innovative preservation and interpretation methods. Virtual reality reconstructions of furnace sites allow visitors to experience these industrial marvels as they once were, even at locations where little physical evidence remains. Oral history projects, utilizing digital archives and interactive displays, ensure that the voices of those who lived and worked in the iron region are preserved for future generations.

Environmental Legacy

The environmental impact of the iron industry continues to shape the region today. While the forests have largely reclaimed the land once cleared for charcoal production, the effects of mining and iron smelting linger. Efforts to remediate polluted soils and waterways are ongoing, with some former industrial sites being transformed into nature preserves and wildlife habitats.

The Wayne National Forest, which encompasses much of the former iron region, stands as a testament to nature's resilience and the potential for ecological restoration. Reforestation projects and wildlife conservation efforts have turned what was once a heavily industrialized landscape into a haven for biodiversity.

Today, the Hanging Rock Iron Region stands at the intersection of past and present, its industrial legacy etched into the landscape and the collective memory of its communities. From hidden ruins in dense forests to carefully preserved historical sites, the remnants of the iron industry continue to fascinate and educate visitors about this crucial chapter in American history.

As we look to the future, the challenge lies in balancing preservation with progress, finding ways to honor the region's industrial heritage while adapting to the needs of the 21st century. The story of the Hanging Rock Iron Region is far from over; it continues to evolve, shaped by the same spirit of innovation and resilience that fueled its furnaces over a century ago.

In the whisper of wind through abandoned casting houses and the crackle of fires at living history demonstrations, we can still hear the echoes of the iron age that forged not just metal, but the very character of this remarkable region.

At sites like Buckeye Furnace, painstakingly restored to its 19th-century appearance, visitors can step back in time and experience the sights, sounds, and even smells of a working iron furnace. Interpretive centers and living history demonstrations bring the past to life, allowing new generations to connect with the experiences of their forebears. But preservation efforts extend beyond the physical remains of the iron industry. Oral history projects capture the memories of those who lived and worked in the region during its industrial heyday, ensuring that the personal stories and everyday experiences of ordinary people are not lost. These narratives, rich in detail and emotion, provide a human context to the broader historical narrative, reminding us that history is not just about events and processes, but about people.

The legacy of the Hanging Rock Iron Region also lives on in the skills and traditions passed down through generations. The craftsmanship that once went into operating a blast furnace or laying a section of rail has found new expression in the work of local artisans and craftspeople. Blacksmiths, woodworkers, and other skilled artisans continue to practice trades that have their roots in the region's industrial past, keeping alive traditional techniques while adapting them to contemporary needs.

As we look to the future, the Hanging Rock Iron Region offers valuable lessons for our changing world. The story of this region is a reminder of the complex interplay between human industry and the natural environment, the importance of community in the face of challenges, and the power of human ingenuity and adaptability.

The rise and fall of the iron industry in this region mirrors broader patterns of industrial development and decline that continue to shape our world today. As we grapple with the challenges of economic transition, environmental sustainability, and community resilience, we would do well to look to the example of those who came before us in the Hanging Rock Iron Region. They teach us about the importance of respecting and stewarding our natural resources, of building strong communities that can weather economic ups and downs, and of never losing sight of the human element in the midst of technological and industrial change. These lessons are as relevant today as they were a century and a half ago, offering guidance as we navigate our own era of rapid change and uncertainty.

Moreover, the story of the Hanging Rock Iron Region reminds us of the power of place - how the landscape we inhabit shapes us even as we shape it, and how our connection to the land and to each other forms the bedrock of our identities and communities. In an age of increasing mobility and digital connectivity, there is something profound and grounding in the deep sense of place that characterizes this region.

As our journey through the history of the Hanging Rock Iron Region comes to a close, we are left with a sense of awe at the achievements of those who came before us, and a deep appreciation for the legacy they have left behind. The furnaces may be silent now, the company towns largely gone, but the spirit of this place lives on - in the stories passed down through generations, in the skills and values inherited from iron-working ancestors, and in the very landscape itself.

The next time you drive through the rolling hills of southern Ohio, northern Kentucky, or western West Virginia, take a moment to listen.

In the rustle of leaves, in the murmur of streams, in the whisper of wind through abandoned furnace stacks, you might just hear the echoes of the Hanging Rock Iron Region's past. And in those echoes, you'll find not just the story of iron and industry, but a testament to the enduring strength of the human spirit and the unbreakable bonds of community.

For in the end, it is not the iron that forms the true legacy of this region, but the indomitable will of its people - a will as strong and enduring as the very metal they once forged. It is this legacy, burnished by time and tempered by experience, that continues to shape the Hanging Rock Iron Region today, and that will guide it into whatever future lies ahead.

As the sun sets on our exploration of this remarkable chapter in American history, we are reminded that the story of the Hanging Rock Iron Region is far from over. It continues to unfold in the lives of those who call this region home, in the ongoing efforts to preserve its heritage, and in the lessons it offers to a world grappling with many of the same challenges that faced the iron workers of yesteryear.

May we carry with us the spirit of the Hanging Rock Iron Region - its resilience, its sense of community, its respect for the land, and its capacity for reinvention. For in that spirit, we find not just a reflection of our past, but a beacon to light our way forward.

Buckeye Furnace

Buckeye Furnace

An example of **scrip** used in the second half of the 19th century. This is from Richland Furnace and was legal tender at the company store.

Lawrence Furnace

Lawrence Furnace

Union Furnace. All photos undated.

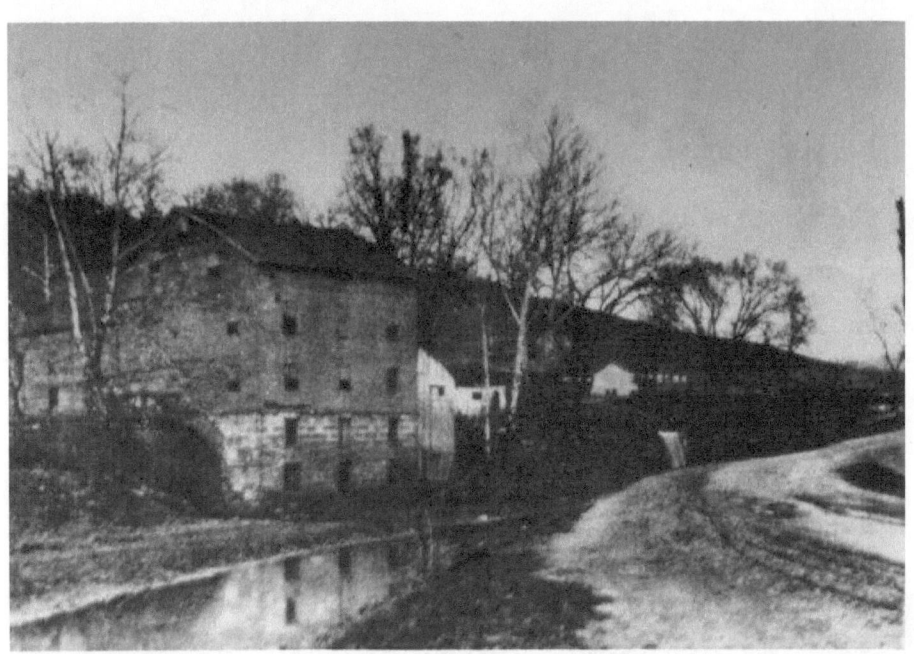

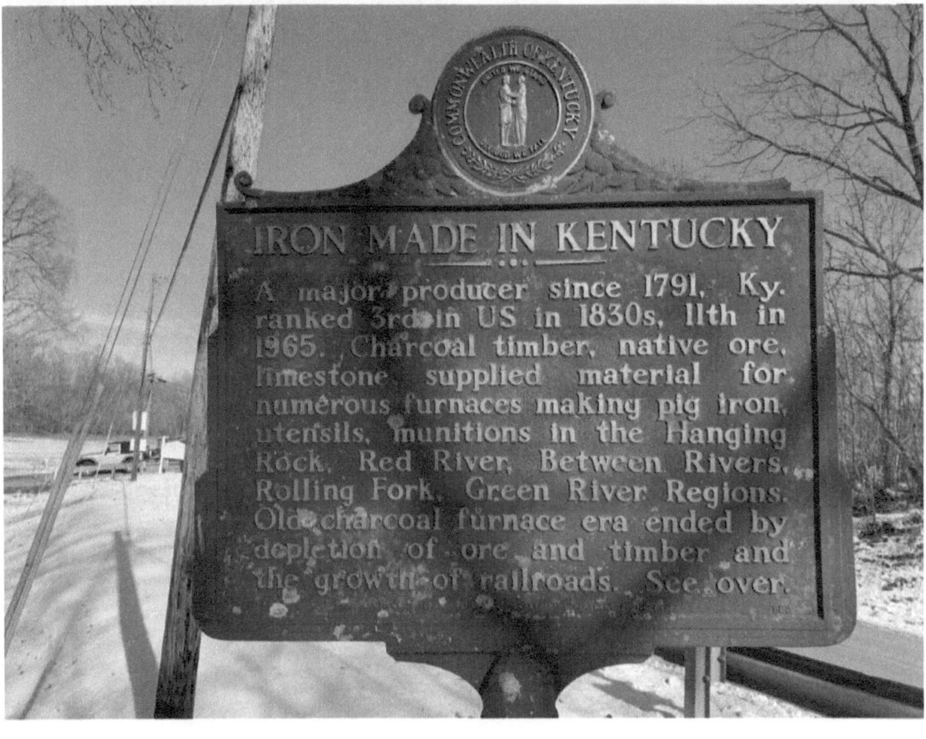
COMMONWEALTH OF KENTUCKY
IRON MADE IN KENTUCKY
A major producer since 1791, Ky.
ranked 3rd in US in 1830s, 11th in
1965. Charcoal timber, native ore,
limestone supplied material for
numerous furnaces making pig iron,
utensils, munitions in the Hanging
Rock, Red River, Between Rivers,
Rolling Fork, Green River Regions.
Old charcoal furnace era ended by
depletion of ore and timber and
the growth of railroads. See over.

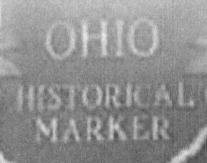

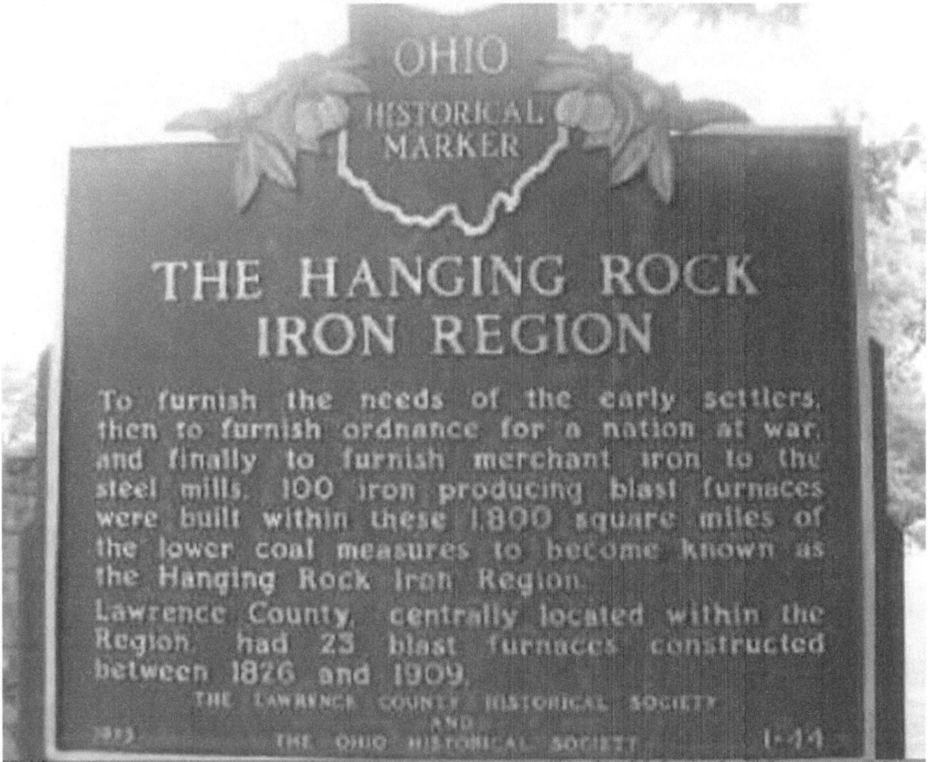
OHIO
HISTORICAL
MARKER
THE HANGING ROCK
IRON REGION
To furnish the needs of the early settlers, then to furnish ordnance for a nation at war, and finally to furnish merchant iron to the steel mills, 100 iron producing blast furnaces were built within these 1,800 square miles of the lower coal measures to become known as the Hanging Rock Iron Region.
Lawrence County, centrally located within the Region, had 23 blast furnaces constructed between 1826 and 1909.
THE LAWRENCE COUNTY HISTORICAL SOCIETY
AND
THE OHIO HISTORICAL SOCIETY
1-44

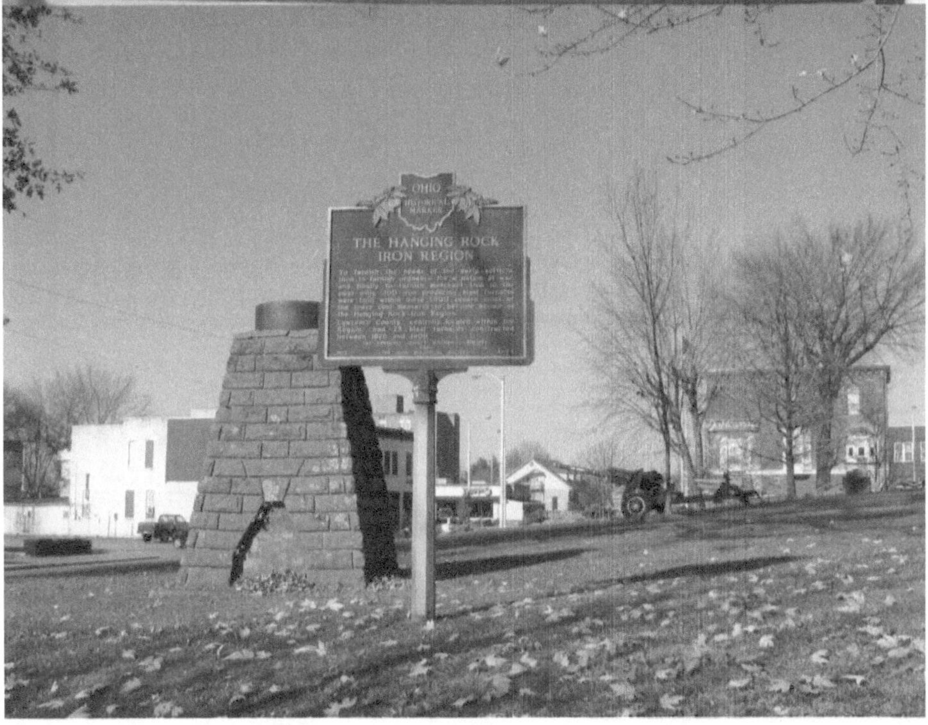
OHIO
HISTORICAL
MARKER
THE HANGING ROCK
IRON REGION

Readers will be surprised with the region's iron furnace locations correlating with mounds and earthworks of the same area. An upcoming book will take a closer look at the links between prehistoric mounds and the links to these furnaces. –Dr. Mackey

Embark on a Journey through the Heart of the Hanging Rock Iron Region

Discover the remnants of a bygone era where molten iron flowed and industry thrived. Explore the historical sites and natural beauty of the Hanging Rock Iron Region, a testament to Ohio's rich industrial heritage.

Featured Destinations:

1. **Buckeye Furnace State Memorial, Wellston, Ohio**

- **GPS Coordinates:** 39.1230° N, 82.4906° W
- **Highlights:** Reconstructed charcoal-fired blast furnace, museum exhibits on the iron-making process, scenic hiking trails through the surrounding forest.
-

Buckeye Furnace, Ohio

2. **Hope Furnace, Lake Hope State Park, Ohio**

- **GPS Coordinates:** 39.4491° N, 82.3821° W
- **Highlights:** Ruins of the Hope Furnace stack, historical marker detailing Ohio's Hanging Rock Iron Region, tranquil setting within Lake Hope State Park, opportunities for hiking, fishing, and camping.
-

Hope Furnace, Ohio

3. **Scioto Furnace, Sciotoville, Ohio**

- **GPS Coordinates:** 38.7519° N, 82.8488° W
- **Highlights:** Remains of the Scioto Furnace stack and other structures, interpretive signage explaining the furnace's history and operation, access to the Ohio River, nearby hiking and biking trails.

Scioto Furnace, Ohio

4. **Vesuvius Furnace, Lawrence County, Ohio**

- **GPS Coordinates:** 38.5816° N, 82.5977° W
- **Highlights:** Picturesque ruins of the Vesuvius Furnace stack, remnants of the furnace complex, scenic location along Storms Creek, opportunities for hiking and exploring the surrounding natural areas.

Vesuvius Furnace, Ohio

5. **Buckhorn Furnace, Lawrence County, Ohio**

- **GPS Coordinates:** 38.6695° N, 82.5959° W
- **Highlights:** Remnants of the Buckhorn Furnace stack and other structures, located near the scenic Lake Vesuvius, opportunities for hiking, fishing, and enjoying the outdoors.

Buckhorn Furnace, Ohio

Additional Nearby Furnace Sites to Explore:

- **Center Furnace, Lawrence County, Ohio**
- **Hecla Furnace, Lawrence County, Ohio**
- **Union Furnace, Lawrence County, Ohio**
- **Hanging Rock Furnace, Scioto County, Ohio**
- **Franklin Furnace, Scioto County, Ohio**

Plan Your Adventure Today:

Immerse yourself in the history and natural beauty of the Hanging Rock Iron Region. Discover the remnants of a once-thriving industry, hike through picturesque landscapes, and experience the unique charm of this remarkable region.

Remember:

- Check the operating hours and accessibility of each site before your visit.
- Respect the historical sites and leave no trace.
- Be prepared for outdoor activities with appropriate clothing, footwear, and supplies.
- Pray to the Lord Jesus Christ if entering an area known to contain mounds.
- Enjoy your journey through the heart of the iron heritage!